More Advance Praise

This book shares essential lessons from one of history's giants juxtaposed with concrete examples from contemporary lean leaders and punctuated with thoughtful questions and reflection. Jerry's book inspires and inquires.

Bruce Hamilton
President, GBMP, Inc.

Jerry brings together lessons from modern day leaders, but with an interesting twist – comparisons to our 16th president! A refreshing perspective, a must-read for all current and aspiring lean leaders.

Helen Zak
President and COO, ThedaCare Center for Healthcare Value

Lean can switch on people power, but only if senior leaders generate the juice. That is a big chunk of the responsibility of a lean CEO, but not the only one. A lean CEO must herd others through a clear mission and objectives. This is leadership of people, not financial or statistical abstractions, and it goes well beyond leadership standard work.

Bussell writes from the view of a practitioner, nicely illustrating the behavior and beliefs of a lean CEO – and the inevitable slip-ups. He tells his own leadership stories and that of several others so it is a fast read, not bogged in rule-based prescription.

Robert W. "Doc" Hall
Author, *Zero Inventory*
and *Compression: Meeting the Challenges of Sustainability Through Vigorous Learning Enterprises*
Founder, Association for Manufacturing Excellence
Former editor, *Target* magazine

Jerry Bussell marshals wisdom on lean leadership that can come only from actual experience, embedded with a deep understanding of principled leadership. As a result of deep reflection, Jerry powerfully illustrates how an effective lean leader is built.

Jim Huntzinger
President, Lean Frontiers

This is a must-read for all operational leaders. In a time when the talk is mostly about pushing the decision making as low in the organization as possible, we forget about the importance of leadership. Jerry has intelligently linked these timeless leadership principles with the past and present in a way to challenge and encourage our leaders of the future and today.

Craig Long
Vice President, Performance Solutions by Milliken

After over 30 years of being a student and practitioner of lean, it eventually became obvious to me that the most important task was to create a culture of continuous improvement and that the key to that task is specific leadership behaviors. Jerry Bussel's new book has given us a deep dive into true lean leadership.

George Koenigsaecker
Board Member, Simpler Holdings, Inc.

This book clearly shows that a Lean or Toyota leader is not vested in individual acts of self-interest (egoism), but rather on collective acts of altruism of the holistic system of company, people and standard processes. The golden rule, albeit never mentioned, is a common stream in every chapter utilizing numerous CEOs and one of America's greatest presidents. A must-read for true north lean leadership.

Ross E. Robson
President & CEO, DnR Lean LLC
Strategic Creator & Executive Director (retired), Shingo Prize

This book is anchored with examples of qualities that strong leaders demonstrate during successful transformational journeys. It is a practical orientation to the lean process, filled with specific executive characteristics that reminds and challenges us to adopt new habits as we lead.

David C. McKinley
President, Henry Schein Medical

ANATOMY

OF A

LEAN

LEADER

as ILLUSTRATED by

10 MODERN CEOs

and ABRAHAM LINCOLN

Jerry Bussell
with
Emily Adams

Published by UL LLC.
333 Pfingsten Rd.
Northbrook, IL. 60062

UL and the UL logo are trademarks of UL LLC.

Printed and bound in the United States of America

ISBN: 978-0-9859370-0-3

Library of Congress Control Number: 2012947081

Editor: James P. Womack
Copy Editor: Laurie Anderson
Jacket Design: Tom Adams
Interior Book Design: Durable Goods Studio

To my wife Mary, daughter Brianne and son James for their unconditional love, encouragement and support.

And in loving memory of my brother Brian Neil Bussell (1954 -2009) who urged me to write this book and was always there for me when I needed his help.

Contents

INTRODUCTION

One of the most difficult things a person can attempt is to lead a group of people in a unified course of action. Whether the leader is a basketball coach, grade-school teacher or a Fortune 500 chief executive, the dilemma is the same: how to inspire people to do their best possible work, using their own skills and energy toward a common cause.

Over the course of 30-plus years in business leadership positions, I have seen plenty of people do this badly. I have seen executives bully their way through delicate situations, lay down laws, or hide behind layers of management and call it leadership. Even when bad management got results, however, nobody could mistake it for leadership. True leadership is rare and, for me, it was a little like art - hard to define, but I knew it when I saw it and was always inspired.

Because my career has been largely focused on transforming businesses using lean thinking, the question of leadership in this unique environment became a life-long fascination. Lean businesses, after all, have special leadership requirements. Before we go into those requirements, however, let's define lean thinking. I assume that readers of this book have a pretty good understanding of lean, but there are many programs and initiatives out there that claim to be *lean* while not reading from the same page. So, let's have a common definition. My friend Jim Womack, who coined the term *lean thinking* along with his co-author Dan Jones in the book by the same name, defines lean this way:

> *Lean thinking is an organization-wide strategy that focuses on delivering ever more value, as defined by the customer, through continuous improvement of processes to eliminate waste. Lean does this by engaging people at all levels of the organization every day to improve their work and their work experience for the benefit of the customer.*

Introduction

In a customer-centric organization such as this, where everyone is actively engaged in improving processes and delivering more value to the customer, the power structure is – or should be – upside down. The most important people are the front-line workers who make the goods or provide the services that the customer desires. The leader is in service to everyone actually making the product, as well as to the customer. Even junior team members can be called upon to lead continuous improvement teams that might include all levels of management.

In a lean business, everyone in the company inhabits the same ecosystem. We work to create a continuous, open loop of improvement that feeds off the knowledge and skills of everyone in the organization. Managing by fiat or shutting down the opinions of others is a poison to the system. In this environment true leadership is not a nicety; it is a necessity.

After years spent studying great leaders, visiting lean organizations around the world and leading large organizations, I began presenting what I knew of leadership at conferences. In conversation with others, I further honed my understanding of great leadership into the 10 characteristics of a lean leader. A successful lean leader must be:

- Purposeful
- Respectful
- Transparently honest
- An influencer
- A continuous learner
- Persistent
- A holistic thinker
- A problem solver
- Results-driven
- Courageous

Fortunately, these characteristics can be acquired. All it takes is knowledge, the desire to adopt new habits and willingness to accept feedback from others. Before diving in to a full discussion of each of these characteristics and how they apply to a lean organization, however, I should offer some background – the building blocks of these ideas.

Beginning in the early 1990s while studying for my MBA - and already incorporating lean ideas into an Allergan, Inc. site in Waco, Texas, where I was managing director - I searched for the magic recipe that could make an ordinary person into a leader. My studies took me from the contemporary leadership theories of Warren Bennis and Stephen Covey to great leaders and thinkers such as Socrates and Abraham Lincoln.

From Bennis and Covey, I learned to search deeper for leadership than mere behaviors. In his classic, *On Becoming a Leader*, Bennis outlined four essential competencies. Every leader, he wrote, must be able to create shared meanings, have a distinctive voice - which mostly involves revealing one's true self - and display integrity. The most important trait, he attested, was adaptive capacity: the ability to relentlessly and intelligently change.[1]

In books and workshops, Covey taught me to lead based on timeless principles such as honesty, courage and humility. Principles drive behavior, Covey asserted, and we need to lead from that deep core instead of simply demanding certain conduct. Having studied for the priesthood as a young man, where I searched for my true purpose in life, these lessons resonated with me. Leadership was not so much about the words we used or the business theories we espoused; it was about acting from the basis of our moral values, from an unshakeable foundation of integrity.

This style of leadership not only felt right, it got results. Following training in Covey's *7 Habits*,[2] I saw my team become more engaged and enthusiastic, offering ideas about improvement and bringing fresh energy to the cause. Still, I knew I was only scratching the surface.

In reading about the lives of Socrates and President Abraham Lincoln, I

---

1. Warren Bennis is the founding chair of the University of Southern California Leadership Institute and widely considered a pioneer in studies on leadership. Bennis has written 30 books and one of them, *On Becoming a Leader* (Perseus Books, 1989), was designated by the *Financial Times* as one of the top 50 business books of all time.
2. In 2002 *Forbes* magazine named Stephen Covey's book, *The 7 Habits of Highly Effective People* (Free Press, 1989) one of the top ten most influential management books ever.

could see this kind of principled leadership in action. Lincoln's ability to knit together a nation at odds and free it from slavery, and Socrates' commitment to engaging people to find answers on their own by using reason, was inspirational. The lives of these men were illustrations of the very thing I was trying to understand. Through the years, I collected biographies and stories, trying to understand the common traits that made them great leaders. I wanted to find the formula.

By 1998, I was practicing continuous improvement as director of Operations at the surgical supply manufacturing company, Xomed Surgical Products, Inc. My knowledge of continuous improvement was limited, but I read the books I could find and trained my team using Covey's *7 Habits* and the ideas of the Toyota Production System. This mash-up was getting great results. The customer fill rate – our percentage of orders filled and shipped on time – jumped from 75 percent to 99. Quality was up and costs were down. But it was a home brew.

What we needed, CEO Jim Treace told me, was an organizing model for world-class operations. He gave me one year to research the best improvement systems and find a good fit for Xomed. Eight months later, I was running out of time and discouraged when a brochure for the Shingo Prize Conference crossed my desk. It was there I realized just how much I did not know about lean thinking.

In one presentation after another, I saw companies struggling with common problems and making incredible leaps in performance through the application of lean. In the hallways, my team just looked at me. I thought we were doing great things at Xomed, but I was wrong. "Great" was still a long way off.

More than the tools and results, what really impressed me among the lean organizations were the leaders. I met CEOs like Art Byrne and George Koenigsaecker who not only knew the lean tools, they were teaching these tools to others. Byrne was already widely known as one of the original lean pioneers in the U.S. and had taken a small, struggling company that made electrical wire management products in Hartford, Connecticut, and transformed it into an international powerhouse, increasing its value by 2,467 percent. Koenigsaecker had a hand in successfully transforming 12 companies to lean thinking and has been called the "Johnny Appleseed of Lean" by *IndustryWeek* magazine.[3] These two were frequently on shop floors, teaching others the tools of lean. Leaders I knew delegated such activities. To be fair, I delegated too. I was not immersed in the improvement activities. I might have offered to help with a task – so long as someone came to me asking a question. But these leaders, they were out on the floor asking operators what help they needed. They were of service to the individuals, the organization and the customer. In short, these leaders were modeling behavior I had not seen before – although I had read about it in some of those Lincoln biographies.

In 1863, for instance, when General Robert E. Lee was holding the state of Virginia and attacking the North mercilessly from this stronghold, Lincoln sat down to write a letter to one of his generals in the field. Major General Joseph Hooker had been out-flanked by Gen. Lee at Chancellorsville and forced to retreat just weeks earlier. In the letter of June 16, 1863, it is apparent that Lincoln is both trying to bolster Hooker's flagging spirits and mediate a dispute between Hooker and General-in-Chief Henry Halleck when he wrote:

> *As it looks to me, Lee's now returning toward Harper's Ferry gives you back the chance that I thought (Maj. Gen. George) McClellan lost last fall. Quite possibly I was wrong both then and now; but, in the great responsibility resting upon me, I cannot be entirely silent. Now, all I ask is that you will be in such mood that we can get into our action the best cordial judgment of yourself and General Halleck, with my poor mite added, if indeed he and you shall think it entitled to any consideration at all.*[4]

Note how Lincoln places his opinions – and his ego – firmly in service to his generals, and the greater war effort. The more I read about leadership at Toyota during the great quality push in the 1950s and 1960s, I more I saw the same sensibility. Executives were constantly at *gemba*[5] looking to serve the greater efforts of the company.

---

3. Both Art Byrne and George Koenigsaecker have written worthy books on leading lean transformations. The titles can be found in the bibliography.

4. David Acord, *What Would Lincoln Do?* (Sourcebooks, Inc. 2009) 124

5. Gemba is a Japanese word that is used to refer to shop floors or any place that value is being

Introduction

At that first conference, I bought a book on value stream mapping and went back to Jacksonville, Florida, with my team, looking to implement what we knew. With the full backing of Xomed's board and executives, my team and I set about recreating operations in the spirit of lean. Failure was my best teacher. In those early, heady weeks, my team and I organized operations into value streams, looked at our available personnel and simply plugged people into roles. We did not ask people what they wanted or what they believed their strengths to be. It was disrespectful and a violation of the second characteristic of a lean leader. It was not long before our efforts were in disarray. We learned, however, and continued forward.

Later that same year – 1999 – Medtronic Inc. bought Xomed and I began learning the true value of *purpose*. Medtronic's mission was to "Alleviate pain, restore health, extend life," and these intentions were central to every effort. At annual gatherings, patients and families were flown in to talk with us about how Medtronic products affected their lives. I learned to serve the purpose first and joined more improvement teams – not as a leader, but as a team member, pulling together with my colleagues to improve lives.

As Medtronic's lean work in Jacksonville became known, we hosted a lot of visiting companies and toured others in turn, always learning by example. I took a trip to Japan to study leadership there and saw a level of trust between executives and operators that was unparalleled. In the best companies, people were not fired for poor performance. Instead, leaders saw it as their personal responsibility to find the best fit, job-wise, for the person. Poor performance was the fault of the teacher as much or more than the pupil. I also saw peer-to-peer disagreements that would get so heated as to nearly create fistfights. This was because nobody walked away in seething disagreement. Consensus was the goal.

Flying high over the Pacific Ocean after one such trip, I realized that the leadership style I saw at Toyota and other world-class Japanese companies mirrored that of Lincoln. In fact, I was reading Shigeo Shingo's *Kaizen and the Art*

---

created for a customer, whether internal or external. Gemba means "the place where value is created."

of Creative Thinking, when I realized that he was a student of Lincoln, as well. In this book, Shingo tells a story from the Battle of Antietam, September 1862, just 18 months into Lincoln's presidency. Lincoln had ordered Maj. Gen. George McClellan – known for his reluctance to engage Confederate troops – to meet Robert E. Lee's Army of Northern Virginia before it could invade Washington, D.C. McClellan was stalling, again, despite the fact that his troops outnumbered the Southern army.

> *"Lincoln was contemplating how he could break this stalemate when an anecdote from his childhood sprang to mind.*
>
> *One day as a young child, he was having trouble putting on his long sock. Even though he was pulling hard, his feet would not go in smoothly and the socks kept snagging on his toes.*
>
> *Seeing him struggle, his mother came to help him. She rolled his socks inside out, put his foot in one of them, and then rolled it up.*
>
> *"What I need to do is reverse the socks," Lincoln thought. He went back to his subordinate and said, "General, you said two in the defense is worth three in the offense. That means you can defend against the enemy with two-thirds of your troops. Therefore, I will give you 29,000 troops to be used for defensive measures here. The other 58,000 I will take with me and go on the offensive to disrupt the enemy."*
>
> *The timid Gen. McClellan blanched at this idea and reluctantly set off to meet Gen. Lee. In this way, Lincoln used the method of reverse thinking to solve his problem and break his stalemate with McClellan."[6]*

What struck me on that flight, reading this anecdote, was the way in which one great leader was still restlessly looking for inspiration from other great leaders. And the parallels between the two were staggering. Lincoln and Shingo both believed absolutely in going to where the action was, focusing their actions on a higher purpose, serving people, and telling stories to influence people instead of dictating behaviors. Lincoln went to battlefields, focused his efforts on preserving the union of the states, helping his subordinates achieve their best work, and spinning tales to illustrate his point. Shingo did the same. He just worked on a factory floor instead of the fields of history.

---

6. Shigeo Shingo, *Kaizen and the Art of Creative Thinking* (Enna Products Corporation, 2007) 113-114

Introduction

When I retired from Medtronic in 2011, I realized that I had been studying leaders – and stealing from them – for 30 years. While I had been giving presentations on leadership in a lean environment for nearly a decade, I realized that I had not taken the time to think deeply and organize what I had learned – to give back. This book is my attempt to do that.

Leading in a lean environment is fundamentally different than any other kind of leadership. Lean work requires that everyone have or develop a healthy dissatisfaction with the status quo. We encourage rebels. Giving orders runs against the grain, even though leaders must get everyone moving in the same direction. The lean business requires a different skill set from its leaders, who must be servants as much as spearheads.

In the style of Socrates translated through one of the great tools of the Toyota Production System, I have ended each chapter with five questions for the lean leader to reflect upon. These questions are similar to the "Five Whys,"[7] in which we attempt to scrape away our assumptions in order to see the root cause of a problem. Here, the questions are more often beginning with "How" or "When" than "Why" because we are not looking for a single root cause. These questions are tools to help leaders look deeper into their habits and motivations.

Like the stories from ten modern leaders contained in the chapters ahead, I hope that these questions will open new avenues of insight. The job of a leader is wider and deeper than I ever imagined at the beginning of my career. May your experience be deeper still.

---

7. Another tool of the Toyota Production System, in which a team considers a circumstance or defect and asks *why* five times – each question more focused – until the root cause is discovered.

PURPOSE

Acting with purpose is straightforward for an individual. Having decided on a course of action, one simply moves ahead with confidence. Leading an organization of any size, however, requires a broader definition of the word.

For leaders, being purposeful means finding both the emotional and the market definition of the group's highest purpose, putting it in human terms, and turning everyone to face in that direction. Does that sound like a tall order? Consider the story of my former colleague, Keith Williams.[8]

At Medtronic, Keith served as president of the Asia-Pacific Group, of the Spinal and Neurological Business Unit and in other leadership positions. He knew how to lead. But when he took the job as president of UL (Underwriters Laboratories) in 2005, he was joining a company that was both set in its ways and in desperate need of change.

For 110 years before Keith arrived, the not-for-profit UL set safety standards for electrical equipment and provided testing and certification. A search of any home or office will turn up dozens - or hundreds - of the UL seals of approval. For 90 of its years, UL had operated virtually without competition, but the rise of the global economy brought new players to market.

UL had suffered a fair amount of trauma before Keith joined as its 10th president. There had been restructuring and downsizing; the former CEO had been asked to leave; the sense of mission had grown distorted. UL's entrenched business practices often made their response times slow or the cost of services

---

8. In my role as executive advisor to UL's Center for Continuous Improvement and Innovation, I still was working with Keith Williams at the writing of this book.

too high. Yet, Keith had his eye on more profound changes to the culture of UL.

This was crystallized for Keith when, just a few of months into his tenure, he attended a meeting of the top 120 company leaders. During a break in proceedings, Keith remembered, "A guy said to me, 'Keith, the people who work for me are afraid of me, and that's the way I like it.' I realized this was not one guy, this was a statement of the kind of command-and-control culture that was entrenched at UL."

This type of leadership was not unusual, but it troubled Keith. His job was to bring UL into the 21st Century and he wanted to start recruiting the best and brightest engineers – people who would help make UL into the global, flexible, collaborative organization he envisioned.

"The trouble was, I knew that young people had grown up online, with social media. They were accustomed to collaborating with peers, to using connectivity to their benefit. We needed them. But I could not imagine recruiting them into this environment," Keith said.

The sticking points were the command-and-control management and regionalism. The UL of 2005 was set up so that every testing laboratory was an independent profit-and-loss center. There was no incentive to share workloads. One lab could be idle while another had serious backlogs. Labs competed with one another; sometimes undercutting the prices of other UL labs and then making customers wait for that seal of approval. The hierarchical nature of management meant there was little or no training offered because, who wants to train their replacement?

Here is why I think of Keith as an embodiment of *purposeful*: He needed to make several changes at once, but knew that it needed to be coherent. So, he linked every initiative and structural change to a central idea – the organization's true purpose – and communicated it very personally in weekly letters to all employees.

Those weekly missives should be required reading for leaders. Personable and sometimes chatty, the letters invited all employees into Keith's confidence. He wrote about laboratories he visited, people he met, and new opportunities he saw. From his first week on the job, Keith laid out his own purpose, writing: "With our Public Safety mission as the foundation for all we do, I came to UL with these basic principles: teamwork, trust and transparency."

Within a few weeks, he announced that Operations would no longer be judged by profit and loss, that UL was launching a lean initiative, and that accounting practices were changing to more accurately reflect cost and revenue. When announcing that last change, he wrote, "We're not here to make money – we're here to promote Public Safety."

Soon, he was busy pulling people into a rewrite of UL's mission statement, to update and highlight the organization's purpose. Drafts were circulated and discussed until everyone knew the boiled-down version: to promote safe living and working environments for people. This was a mission that everyone could rally behind – keeping people safe.

This is not to say that UL or its CEO had just one purpose. None of us live without competing interests – various initiatives clamor for our attention; decisions need to be made about a dozen critical issues right now.

Just like Abraham Maslow[9] identified a hierarchy of human needs, leaders must identify their hierarchy of purpose. Companies need to make money, produce quality products and keep customers and employees happy. But one purpose must unite all efforts. Keith believed strongly in teamwork, trust and transparency – as can be seen in his commitment to communication and transformation through lean teamwork – but those principles are in service to the organization's higher calling: keeping people safe.

---

9. American professor of psychology at universities such as Columbia and Brandeis, Maslow was interested in how people became successful and pioneered research into psychological health, as opposed to illness. Best known for his theory on the hierarchy of needs, Maslow stated that people must have basic needs met such as nutrition and adequate sleep before they could focus on higher needs such as intellectual stimulation.

Purpose

"If you talk about your purpose all the time, which we do, it becomes a checkpoint for decisions," Keith said. "When people wanted to preserve the dysfunctional culture, we kept coming back to the purpose. 'Why are we here? To promote safe living.' Just asking the question changes the debate. If you have a mission that embodies your true intentions, you can use that to elevate discussions.

"Promoting safety has become the foundation of every question we consider – acquisitions, policy, everything."

About 31 years before UL came into existence, this nation and its president were struggling with similar issues. In the midst of a civil war, when the nation was being ripped apart and slavery was the core of fierce debates, what was a leader's priority?

In the dark days of 1862, Abraham Lincoln was having real difficulty getting his generals to engage the Confederate Army. Several border states were teetering on the brink of secession and Lincoln, who had sworn to lead the United States as a unified nation, faced his own hierarchy of purpose.

Lincoln was opposed to slavery down to his bones. In his first of his famous debates with U.S. Senator Stephan A. Douglas in 1858, Lincoln made his position clear saying there was "no reason in the world why the negro is not entitled to all the natural rights enumerated in the Declaration of Independence, the right to life, liberty and the pursuit of happiness ... in the right to eat the bread, without the leave of anyone else, which his own hand earns, he is my equal and the equal of Judge Douglas, and the equal of every living man."

Yet, nearly two years after taking the oath of office, Lincoln had not attempted any policy or law to free the slaves, even though many were held in Union states. I can only imagine how this would have eaten at his conscience. Finally, with the Preliminary Emancipation Proclamation, he declared that all slaves *living outside of the Union states* would be free as of January 1, 1863. That meant slaves in New York, Pennsylvania and Missouri, for instance, would still be held. Why?

No matter how personally repugnant Lincoln found the institution of slavery, he had pledged to lead the *United States*. His first purpose was to hold the nation together. In his first inaugural address, Lincoln was most eloquent on this point, telling leaders of the Southern rebellion:

> *We are not enemies, but friends. We must not be enemies. Though passion may have strained, it must not break our bonds of affection. The mystic chords of memory, stretching from every battlefield and patriot grave to every living heart and hearthstone all over this broad land, will yet swell the chorus of the Union, when again touched, as surely they will be, by the better angels of our nature.*

Lincoln's hierarchy was *union* first, emancipation a close second. In 1862, believing that he had no constitutional authority to free lawfully held slaves, Lincoln called his Preliminary Emancipation Proclamation a "military measure." Lincoln freed slaves held in Confederate states in order to beef up Union armies. And many slaves fleeing the Southern states did join the Union forces. But slaves held in the North remained in bondage because Lincoln believed the country was not yet ready for the 13th Amendment, the Abolition of Slavery.[10]

Had Lincoln freed every slave in the nation, he risked losing the four border states of Delaware, Maryland, Missouri and Kentucky to the Confederacy. He could have failed in his primary purpose, preserving the United States, in order to push his personal conviction – no matter how moral or dearly held – onto a nation not yet prepared or wholly convinced of its necessity.

The glaze of history makes Lincoln's decision seem simple. But this was a man who had seen the violence and degradation of slavery up close while working on flatboats, taking goods along the Sangamon, Illinois and Mississippi rivers. He had compared his own youth, in which he served as a kind of indentured servant to his own unyielding father, to quasi-slavery.[11] The decision to wait, to only free some slaves, must have been wrenching. But the chaos that could

---

10. The 13th Amendment was presented to the states for ratification in February 1865, just three months before Lincoln's assassination.
11. Lincoln held many jobs in his youth and gave his father, Thomas, all of his earnings until he was 21, as was expected.

have ensued if Lincoln violated the Constitution and lost those border states could have meant the permanent separation of this country into North and South. We should, perhaps, all be grateful that Lincoln respected his higher purpose.

Having a well-defined purpose can make tough decisions a little easier. At the very least, it gives us a shared starting point for decision making and problem solving. As Keith said earlier, having a purpose means having a foundation for every debate – a common lens for viewing the world.

Keith and I both came from the world of Medtronic, where one elegant mission was ever-present as a guide: "Alleviate pain, restore health, extend life." Whether we were allocating resources or deciding on a path forward, this mission – and the people who were being helped by Medtronic products – was always central to our considerations.

When defining his hierarchy of needs, Abraham Maslow said that a person must have the foundational needs met – air, water, food – before he or she could hope for the higher aspirations such as love and self-actualization. We can draw the same pyramid for a modern CEO.

Leaders need to be able to rally the troops, to have people that are willing to follow, to introduce new products and open new markets. But first, he or she needs to present a compelling vision for the company, one that resonates with people, and teach everyone to serve the mission. As Lincoln learned, this can lead to tough decisions no matter how clear the path may seem. How does a leader proceed when he needs to win over the leaders of various sites around the country, even while radically changing the culture to be in service to the mission?

At UL, Keith was moving rapidly ahead with lean training and improvement teams in that first year. He knew that improving response times in the testing labs would benefit UL's safety mission. Yet, introducing lean teams into a command-and-control environment was not going to be easy. Problems soon surfaced.

Within weeks, Keith discovered that some employees were being encouraged to "soft pedal" process problems to representatives of *kaizen*[12] teams seeking to understand the current state. Others were told they could not speak to Keith without prior approval – and screening – by a supervisor. Keith's reaction was swift and public as he wrote in a weekly missive, "Leaders who suppress communication and information flow are inherently weak leaders and will not have a future at the new UL."

Keith needed people on his side. But instead of flattering his leaders or creating a cult of personality, he kept all eyes on the purpose. Over the years, I have adopted one phrase as a kind of personal mantra and it seems to fit here: before ego, purpose.

A few weeks later, when reporting on the first kaizen projects, Keith wrote, "I reminded the change agents that they are not leading change for me or the board; they are leading change for Public Safety, for our customers and for the company where they will want to work for many years until their retirement."

Before ego, purpose.

This is not to say, however, that a company's mission is always worth serving. Because leaders need purpose before reaching for higher goals – such as employee loyalty – some of them mistake mission as a means to an end. These leaders might throw together a mission statement, put it on letterhead and then ignore it entirely or trot it out once a year for a presentation. We know that purpose has been used as a means to an end when the mission statement speaks more to a company's short-term goals than it does to the soul of its people. "Increase shareholder value" is a good example of an ill-considered purpose. Who wants to spend their life's energy working to increase someone else's bank account?

---

12. A Japanese word composed of two characters that translate as "change" and "for the better." In a lean environment, kaizen teams are charged with making substantive improvements to a process within a limited time – usually a week or less.

Purpose

"Shareholder value is a hollow notion as the sole source of employee motivation. If you do business that way, you end up like ITT," Bill George, former CEO of Medtronic, told Lance Secretan for his book *Inspire!* [13]

Shareholder value was not ignored at Medtronic. In fact, from 1985 to 2003, this medical technologies company gave shareholders a return of 32 percent annually.[14] It was a good outcome, but it was not the point. Leaders such as Bill George knew that stock prices were not a good motivator. Helping others to live longer and pain-free, keeping people safe, preserving a union – these are inspirational missions.

Every year at Medtronic, the highlight of the annual party was the people – patients and their families – brought in to tell employees of the effect their work had on lives across the country. Medtronic's business was comprised of six major units supplying doctors with technologies in fields such as cardiac rhythm management and diabetes care. In Medtronic's Jacksonville facility, our business was surgical technologies. So every year, we heard personal tales, often emotional, of lives extended and suffering alleviated through our surgical technologies. We spoke of our mission every day, but at least once a year it again was brought to life.

People were energized and excited after these meetings, but any business leader will have one practical question: What did you do with all that purpose?

We all know that creating enthusiasm around the idea of change can be difficult. Some companies have a burning platform – huge debt, fierce competition, rapidly changing markets – that can be used to encourage everyone to jump into change. At Medtronic, we did not. Business was good. Our products were well received. When I started our lean initiative, I talked endlessly to people about the need for big changes, new systems and fresh ways of looking at problems. I got a lot of blank stares. We were doing fine without lean.

---

13. Lance Secretan, *Inspire! What Great Leaders Do* (John Wiley & Sons, 2004)
14. In the tumultuous market years since 2004, Medtronic's stock prices and dividends have suffered. The most recent CEO responded by assuring investors that shareholder value would be his top priority. This, I believe, will prove to be a mistake.

So, I began studying how other lean organizations had rallied people behind change, and then the theories behind change management. In John Kotter's book, *The Heart of Change*, he described eight steps to creating change and wrote of the need to engage both the left and right sides of the brain. The logic of the left side can only take us so far, he wrote. To truly effect change, we needed to engage the emotional right brain.

This argument made particular sense to me. Having studied Stephen Covey – and sent dozens of people through that training, as well – I knew the positive energy that emotion could create.

Like all good lean thinkers, I also wondered how Toyota Motor Corp. created excitement around change. How did Toyota leaders continue to encourage improvement even as the company was rocketing to the top of car markets around the world? Soon, I came across the original "Toyoda Precepts" written by Kiichiro Toyoda in 1935. The parallels between the Precepts and Medtronic's much shorter mission was quite astonishing. Note the use of emotion and the calling to a higher, human purpose:

1. Be contributive to the development and welfare of the country by working together, regardless of position, in faithfully fulfilling your duties.
2. Be ahead of the times through endless creativity, inquisitiveness and pursuit of improvement.
3. Be practical and avoid frivolity.
4. Be kind and generous; strive to create a warm, homelike atmosphere.
5. Be reverent, and show gratitude for things great and small in thought and deed.

Realizing how emotional I – and others – felt about Medtronic's mission, I knew that our purpose was my best tool to create excitement around improvement.

I spent a lot of time at gemba, walking around, talking to technicians, engineers and operators. I started making it a point to talk about Medtronic's mission. I asked people what the mission meant to them. We would talk about improvement activities, and how kaizen teams helped us make better quality medical devices at lower cost – making them more easily available to people in need. I would ask about family or friends who needed medical products like Medtronic's and then we would talk, again, about how to improve our processes to benefit those family members and friends.

In my travels to various sites, or giving presentations to groups, I made it a point to collect the stories I heard and share them. Following a Chamber of Commerce talk, for instance, in which I spoke of Medtronic and its lean initiative, a young woman approached me with tears in her eyes. She hugged me – a great bear hug – and told me her mother was alive that day because of a Medtronic device. I told that anecdote a lot back in our offices and on the shop floor, always hoping to bring home the hopes and dreams of patients and their families. Stories like this, I discovered, made my point more profoundly than a spreadsheet of Operations data ever could.

It is too easy, sometimes, to lose sight of the larger meaning of our work. Whether a technician or a vice president, we all become immersed in our daily activities, focused on the *what* part of the equation. A good leader, I realized, must keep bringing us back to *why*.

Putting these anecdotes on a bulletin board or in a newsletter, I am convinced, will never have the impact of a heart-felt story, personally delivered. Lean leadership pushes us to be in conversation with the entire organization, to bring the mission to gemba. We all know that the people who work at gemba every day are, in many ways, closer to the customer than executives. They need to be filled with the larger purpose, to ensure that processes and products are always being improved – not because it is their jobs or because they want to impress management, but because they believe in the mission.

I saw plenty of changes in the people of Medtronic during those years. When we focused on helping people, there was real enthusiasm for improvement. But even more apparent to me were the changes I noticed in myself.

Getting people to embrace change is not easy. When I began describing the reason for improvement – in which we ask our people for extra work, additional brainpower – as a higher calling, instead of citing the logic of the lean initiative or passing it off as a personal favor to me, my own attitude changed as well. Lean was not about me or my efforts and hopes and theories anymore. Lean improvements were bigger than I. This was saving lives, not dollars.

The background disagreements in our corporate offices – the turf wars and shifting alliances that are common in any business – mattered less. I felt lighter, more energized, when focused on the well-being of our customers instead of bonus structures and hitting numbers. The mission became my true north.

Five Questions on Purpose

1. What is the true purpose of your company or organization?
2. How do you know that every employee knows your purpose?
3. How do you demonstrate your commitment to this purpose daily?
4. What can you do to influence others in the organizations to become purposeful?
5. What, in your statement of purpose, will motivate people to achieve that purpose without your intervention?

RESPECT

Known as the father of the Japanese industrial revolution, Sakichi Toyoda modernized the weaving industry and pioneered the idea of automatic machine stops in the case of a broken thread. The son of a poor carpenter and by all accounts a modest man of restless intelligence, Toyoda was always seeking to improve on his inventions. He encouraged his son to study loom making outside of Japan, and then supported his interest in automotive manufacturing.

Five years after Sakichi Toyoda's death in 1930, his son Kiichiro Toyoda – who founded the company that would become the global juggernaut, Toyota Motor Corp. – set down what he had learned from his father in a document that became known as the original "Toyoda Precepts". These were to be the underlying principles that would guide the company through nearly a century of growth and change. It will surprise some to know that there is nothing about inventory control, finances, or growth. The first precept:

1. Be contributive to the development and welfare of the country by working together, regardless of position, in faithfully fulfilling your duties.

What does this have to do with respect? Everything.

For years, I have been watching companies flounder or stop short on the meaning of this all-important pillar of lean thinking. Executives say "respect," but then describe simple manners or company picnics. In companies that are still skimming the surface of lean, respect often ends at the Friday report out, when kaizen teams report on the results of improvement efforts. Saying "please" and allowing employees to make improvements are nice – even empowering. Respect, however, reaches far beyond the niceties and follows us home and into our communities.

A respectful leader is in service to the people – to their personal fulfillment and beyond that, to the health, wealth and happiness of the community. Respect means knowing that our words and actions have a profound effect on others, rippling outward to family, schools and other businesses; respect means striving toward positive outcomes for people. Sakichi Toyoda knew that his company – a machine tool manufacturer out in the countryside – affected the entire nation, one employee at a time.

Respect for individuals and their contributions is the way that great companies are built. And respect is essentially how Bob Chapman, chairman and CEO of multi-national manufacturing services and products company Barry-Wehmiller, intends to change the world.

After five years on a lean journey and lots of spectacular results, Bob firmly states that lean is just the technique Barry-Wehmiller Companies, Inc. is using to spread the company's true purpose: the betterment of people. Waste elimination, fewer defects, better quality and output – all of those are great consequences of lean, but metrics are not the point.

Perhaps the best illustration of Bob's point of view is a story from the company's official lean launch for senior executives. For a number of years, Bob had been pushing a leadership program that encouraged interpersonal skills and empowerment, but had failed to get much traction. He hired a lean expert, Dick Ryan, who thought the two initiatives would together generate heat. A few kaizen teams were already at work when senior executives met for the lean unveiling.

Dick Ryan, former president of companies under the Wiremold flag and a self-described lean techie, gave the presentation. There were lots of charts and metrics and projections.

"I got so frustrated at the traditional approach that I put my hands around the lean guy's (Brian Wellinghoff 's) neck and said, 'No wonder 97 out of 100 lean initiatives fail. It's all about numbers'," Bob recounted.

Then, a kaizen team consisting of two UAW[15] workers, a non-union employee and their team leader stood to give a report. Bob listened, unconvinced. How would lean affect people, he wanted to know. Would it touch them at all?

"I asked one of the team members how this kaizen had impacted his life. He thought a second and then said, 'Well, I'm talking to my wife more.' That made me sit back."

Bob asked for an explanation and the team member, Steve, said he had been punching a timecard for a number of years. Nobody asked his opinion. He might get 10 things right, but nobody said anything except on the thing he got wrong. So he went home at night not feeling that great, and maybe, he was not the best husband. But the past week, he had been going home feeling like a person of value. He was nicer to his wife; she talked to him more.

"If we in America are looking at people in our companies as objects to be used toward our success, we are sending people home feeling unappreciated. So they struggle in their marriages, things break apart, our communities lose cohesion," Bob said. "Lean is the most powerful tool I have found to tell people that they matter."

One of Bob's most profound realizations about leadership happened at a wedding. Watching a father give away his daughter in marriage, Bob listened to the man saying that he and his wife gave their daughter to this new husband to have and hold. As the father of six, Bob also heard all that was not said – about the love and care these parents had poured into their child, and how the father was now entrusting his daughter's life and happiness to this man.

"I thought about our employees, how they come to our company from parents that love them and want the best for them. Parents entrust their children to us,

---

15. United Auto Workers

hoping they flourish and become all that is possible. Too often, those children get beaten down."

Respectful leadership, he says, is about guiding people to fulfillment.

Bob knows he sounds like an evangelist. Some people wonder whether he is taking care of business. So, he always begins presentations with a few quick numbers: Barry-Wehmiller is a collection of 70 businesses with 6,000 employees around the world and $1.2 billion in annual revenue. Half of those businesses have been acquired since 1997, which is about when Bob had his first revelation about business being fun and fulfilling for everyone.

Barry-Wehmiller had just acquired a $40 million company that needed help in its customer service department. Bob went in early and unannounced on the first day of ownership to have a cup of coffee. In the break room, a group was talking animatedly about March Madness basketball games and having a lot of fun. As the clock crept closer to 8 a.m. and the starting bell, the energy just drained out of the room, Bob remembered. It made him sad.

He took his cup of coffee to the customer service office and, without thinking about it, announced that they were starting a game. He made it up on the spot. They would play in teams and the person who got the most orders that week would win $100. Every member of the team with the most orders would also win $100. Almost immediately, performance and morale improved dramatically, he said. Teams started vying with each other to give better customer service, return calls and get orders. They would celebrate scores together on Friday evening, and send encouraging text messages back to the one person still in the office writing up orders.

Bob started more games throughout the Barry-Wehmiller companies and began thinking deeply about what motivated people. In 2002, he pulled together a cross-functional team to discuss what they could do to help others achieve. During that meeting, team members wrote the "Guiding Principles of Leadership", with one foundational philosophy, "We measure success by the way we touch the lives of people."

After the lean initiative began, the company launched the Living Legacy of Leadership, or L3, that stated, "We commit to a sustained leadership model that creates a culture where each of us returns home with a sense of fulfillment." The L3 team has representatives from more than a dozen divisions and keeps the company's lean efforts focused on personal fulfillment.

On the heels of L3, leaders created the Barry-Wehmiller University, which offers a three-day communication skills workshop, a two-week L3 skills course and three weeks of training in leadership fundamentals. About 1,000 employees go through one of the classes each year, said Brian Wellinghoff, director of The L3 Journey and the "lean guy" that Chapman playfully choked during the lean kick off.

"Not everyone needs to be a leader, but everyone needs to have an opportunity – not to manage but to inspire, support, and encourage others," Wellinghoff said.

This focus on the culture has had tangible results. Strategy Deployment sessions at the 70 Barry-Wehmiller companies feature no yelling. People are not getting beaten up over their numbers, Dick Ryan said. Instead, these meetings are viewed as an opportunity to help divisions meet goals with the collective intelligence of a team of leaders.

"When we give presentations and talk about Bob Chapman, we get asked, 'Do you guys just sit around celebrating and singing *Kumbaya*?" Ryan said, laughing. "Of course we care about results. The important issue is how we get those results. People aren't beaten up. We aren't making assumptions. We work on asking questions the right way, using the 'Five Whys', and above all, listening."

In my experience, listening is the key to respect and it is important to note that the subtleties of respect will vary from one culture to another. Some companies find a way to show respect and encourage engagement through profit-sharing programs. Others, through games and prizes. The key is to listen and understand what respect looks like from employees' points of view.

Respect

The culture of the Xomed plant in Jacksonville, Florida, for instance, understood respect quite differently from the newly acquired MicroFrance facility in St. Aubin, France.

In Jacksonville, a certain amount of silliness was part of the culture. If leaders held themselves apart from the silliness, it seemed as though we were looking down on fun – and so, down on our employees. The divide between them and us would deepen. That might be alright if we were only looking for employees to respect *us*, but that is not the point when a leader is truly in service to his or her people and their work.

When we wanted to spread lean thinking throughout the facility in Jacksonville, I was lucky enough to hire a talented teacher named Rick Kundert as our Lean Learning manager. Rick believed in physical learning and was a very creative thinker. Knowing that I wanted our people to learn, as opposed to being trained, I encouraged him to find the fun.

The highlight for many was the 5S dance. Rick devised a motion for each of the categories - sort, straighten, sweep, etc. - and made up a little song to go with it. Everyone learned the dance, even me. Now, I am a big guy at six-foot-seven and my Polish heritage leaves me a little rhythm handicapped. I had to practice the dance in front of a mirror to get it right, but I did, and then performed it on shop floors throughout the company and, at least once, in front of an audience of hundreds.

Then Rick, who liked to have his own fun, devised a new game. Everyone got a penny and the goal was to hang on to that penny. At the same time, everyone had to know the 5S dance and do it on request. If the dance was done wrong, the person lost their penny. Of course, management was targeted. That was the fun. I was doing well for a while, until one day when an employee asked for a 5S dance on a shop floor and I tried to rush through the dance, missed a step, and lost my penny. That employee had bragging rights for weeks. And somehow, everyone learned the 5Ss.

That 5S dance was fun, but it just would not fly in France. Fortunately, Xomed actually launched its first lean initiative at the MicroFrance facility – just purchased in 1999 – and the 5S dance was not yet invented, or I might have tried it. It is a frightening thought.

MicroFrance was a family-owned company with about 75 employees housed in a very nice, new building. Nestled in a lovely field in the bucolic town of St. Aubin, MicroFrance made the highest quality surgical instruments for ear, nose, and throat operations. The problem was that lead time for their instruments were 10-12 weeks. After Xomed purchased the company, the initial idea to improve lead time centered on the installation of an MRP system. But then I went to the Shingo Conference, discovered the power of lean, and our plans changed.

The operations manager in St. Aubin, Emmanuel Dujarric, spoke English and helped us figure out how to talk to people about the lean initiative. He also helped me understand French expectations. At Emmanuel's urging, I began every morning at the facility walking through and shaking every employee's hand, looking him or her in the eye and saying, "*Bonjour.*" If I shook the same person's hand twice in a morning, it was a terrible gaff because it meant I was not paying attention. It was a lesson in manners that made me better at really looking at the person to whom I was talking.

We began teaching lean ideas with the paper airplane folding game, where people fold up paper airplanes as individuals and then in teams. We demonstrated the value of workflow, checking quality at every step instead of only at the end, and pull-versus-push demand, and then asked employees for their opinions and ideas. By the time we set about moving their massive machines into the correct order, most everyone was on board and giving helpful advice – even though we made the move during their August shutdown.

Once the operators and managers got comfortable working with the newly lean system, they began posting impressive results toward diminishing lead time. But we quickly found out that this tight group of employees did not like individual recognition. Being singled out made them uncomfortable. If everyone on the team got a shirt that was great. The best way to thank them, however, involved dragging a few tables out into the beautiful field, then serving a little breakfast of bread, pâté and white wine. This is the way French employees felt valued – a kind of celebration that might have caused minor chaos in Jacksonville.

Respect is about listening, but it is also about praise and necessary truth telling. Recognition should not be confined to monthly meetings. For good work and "failed" efforts, recognition should be handed out freely, on the spot. Some of that truth telling can be painful, however. I learned early in my career to save more embarrassing corrections for a private moment.

Lean demands that we give employees the highest respect – giving them the authority to make changes in their work environment (in consultation with others, of course), seeking out their ideas, and giving them the tools to impact the business. This is not always an easy respect to give. Many of us can be guilty of trying to control outcomes, applying pressure to see that our ideas rise to the fore. We can all get pushy, sometimes.

From Emmanuel I learned the value of Socratic method. I cannot count the times I listened to him tell a team member who was reluctant to change, "I am not going to make you do something you don't want to. But would you give me a reason you won't try?" Then, he would work through a few gentle questions about the person's underlying assumptions and hesitancy. Open dialogue is always respectful. Now the senior director of operations for ENT at Medtronic Surgical Technologies, responsible for several manufacturing facilities, Emmanuel became a person I trusted to tell me the truth, even if it was a truth I did not really want to hear.

Honesty is the ultimate respect. Throughout my life and career, I have sought out those who would tell me the truth – about my own behavior and how I affected others, and about whether I was living up to my own standards. There have been many times when my desire to please others, to say "yes" when I should say "no," has left me overcommitted and unable to show others respect by following through on my promises.

My wife, Mary, Emmanuel Dujarric, and Scott Quaratella, director of operations for Medtronic's Mystic, Connecticut, manufacturing facility, were people I turned to frequently when I needed a good dose of the truth. They have asked the same of me and together, we have learned that truth telling and respect are like muscles that need to be worked in order to remain strong. I am fortunate that they continue to have enough respect for me to be honest.

For Abraham Lincoln, trust and respect were far more difficult issues. Those he counted on to be truthful were often rivals with different agendas – as can be true in modern companies, of course. We can learn much from the extent to which Lincoln showed respect for his rivals even in the face of their occasional scorn.

Edwin M. Stanton, Secretary of War, for instance, was Lincoln's opposite: secretive where Lincoln was transparent, impatient and imperious where the president was calm and unruffled. Stanton clashed with the president more than once. Yet Lincoln treated him with a respect above those in his cabinet, rarely vetoing his decisions and almost always reversing his own.[16] Stanton, a Democrat, was widely known for dubbing Lincoln "Original Gorilla" before he joined the president's Republican administration, and his rants continued well into the beginning of the Civil War. But he was slowly converted by Lincoln, who understood Stanton's strengths and praised them whenever possible.

When Stanton snubbed a congressman who had received Lincoln's backing for the War Department's help in a project, Stanton called the president a "damned fool."

> *"Did Stanton say I was a damned fool?" Lincoln asked.*
> *"He did, sir," the congressman replied, and "repeated it."*
> *Lincoln paused, and then remarked, "If Stanton said I was a damned fool then I must be one, for he is nearly always right, and generally says what he means. I will step over and see him."[17]*

Stanton was known to work fifteen-hour days under Lincoln, and the president

---

16. Doris Kearns Goodwin, *Team of Rivals* (Simon & Schuster, 2005) 669
17. Goodwin, *Team of Rivals.* 560

understood that he faced special burdens overseeing the finances and operations of the Union Army. Lincoln would not allow others to heap criticism
on Stanton, even when he defied a presidential order to approve a military
appointment.

"The pressure upon [Stanton] is immeasurable and unending. He is the rock
on the beach of our national ocean against which the breakers dash and roar,
dash and roar without ceasing. He fights back the angry waters and prevents
them from undermining and overwhelming the land. Gentlemen, I do not
see how he survives, why he is not crushed and torn to pieces. Without him I
should be destroyed. He performs his task superhumanly."[18]

Lincoln's secretary of state, William H. Seward, also began his service in the
administration with a low opinion of the president. As Lincoln's chief rival in
the first Republican primary, Seward made it clear he believed he was far better qualified for the nation's top job. Seward tried hard to influence Lincoln's
cabinet selections and when that failed, offered his resignation before Lincoln
could even take the oath of office. Seward attempted to lead the war effort and
secretly met with Confederate leaders over the fate of Fort Sumter. He tried to
convince Lincoln to start a war with another country as a method to unify the
nation and then, when the British ship *Trent* was captured with two Confederate commissioners on board, Seward pushed Lincoln to strike back against
England. "One war at a time," Lincoln responded.[19]

The tension between the two men could have derailed both. But Lincoln soon
made it a habit to drop around Seward's house for long chats. Instead of sum-
moning his secretary of state to the White House, Lincoln went to him, sat in
his parlor and gave Seward his complete attention. The two men enjoyed telling stories and taking carriage rides around Washington, D.C., and within that
first year, found that they had many political views in common.
Known for saying, "I destroy my enemies when I make them my friends," Lin-

---

18. Lincoln made these remarks to two congressmen who sought an appointment to the War
Department that was opposed by Stanton, according to Stanton's biographer, Frank A. Flower.
Flower's book, *Edwin McMasters Stanton*, was published in 1905.
19. Donald T. Phillips, *Lincoln on Leadership: Executive Strategies for Tough Times* (Warner
Books, Inc. 1993) 29

coln was consistently respectful to the two men who were publicly disrespectful to him and, in the end, made them his friends and allies.

In 1861, Seward wrote to his wife, "Executive force and vigor are rare qualities. The president is the best of us."

It is important to remember that Lincoln won over his rivals not through superior arguments or force of will, but with the simple human act of respect. He gave Stanton and Seward his time, his honesty and his esteem. In return, they became his closest and most trusted secretaries.

During Lincoln's time – and earlier, as Industrialism swept through countries – people were managed as if they were machine parts or animate objects. This attitude gained legitimacy with Henry Ford's assembly lines and is still evident in many companies today. The sure sign that employees are being objectified instead of respected is when leaders complain about the difficulties of training and motivating employees, or grumble about their mistakes and attitudes.

Respectful leaders talk about what their employees want, what they are accomplishing, the ideas they bring to the table, and how they are evolving.

The mentality that people are cogs for our giant machines has lasted for hundreds of years, but it is no longer sustainable. People spend 10 hours a day with us; they are expected to do many jobs in a lean company and to acquire skills sets that make them more difficult and costly to replace. We must be different, more respectful leaders in order to create sustainable businesses.

"What we learned through out journey is that people have incredible gifts and when we try to manage people, we suppress those gifts," Bob Chapman said. "Leadership is not managing. Leadership is helping people to become more of who they are supposed to be."

Five Questions on Respect

1. How do you serve your employees?
2. How do your employees (or team) know that you care about their personal fulfillment?
3. How do you get honest and candid feedback from employees about their experience of the job?
4. When other leaders falter in terms of showing respect, how do you find out and how do you correct it?
5. How many employees do you know by first name?

PROBITY

Probity is an old-fashioned word that describes several behaviors. It means transparently honest and, when applied to a person, it refers to someone who holds to the highest principles and ideals. Probity speaks to a person's integrity. Honesty is telling the truth to others; integrity is telling the truth to yourself.

Telling the truth is, regrettably, not the first trait of a leader that springs to mind for people. Business leaders need to be shrewd, to keep their cards close to the vest, right? They need to be sphinxlike in negotiations and guarded in what they say. Some leaders seem to take pride in using many words to say nothing at all substantive.

Are these the traits that inspire trust? Hardly. I would say that the old paradigm of the sphinx leader is rarely useful.[20] In order to lead, we must inspire others to follow and that will not happen without a bond of trust. We win the trust of others through honesty – even when telling the truth is difficult.

Abraham Lincoln, known as "Honest Abe," was also a politician. How much honesty – probity – should we expect from a person in his position? One of my favorite stories about Lincoln's truth telling is found in Donald T. Phillips' popular book *Lincoln on Leadership*. I will paraphrase most of the tale.

Cash-strapped during the Civil War, the story goes, Lincoln asked his secretary of the Treasury, Salmon P. Chase, to issue interest-bearing currency to raise money for the war effort. (These would be legal-tender notes bearing interest at about five percent.) Chase balked, calling the idea unconstitutional.

---

20. Publicly traded companies require a certain amount of discretion from CEOs, of course. But that does not preclude honesty.

Probity

So, Lincoln told Chase the story of an Italian sea captain who ran his ship into a rock and was soon taking on water. While his sailors pumped water out of the hold, the captain went to the bow of the ship and prayed to a statue of the Virgin Mary. The men pumped; the captain prayed, but soon the leak was winning and sinking seemed imminent. The captain, enraged, threw the statue of the Virgin Mary overboard. The water filling the hold slowed and then stopped. The sailors finished pumping and all got safely to port where, in dry dock, they found the statue of the Virgin Mary stuck headfirst in the hole.

"I don't intend precisely to throw the Virgin Mary overboard, and by that I mean the Constitution," Lincoln explained to Chase. "But I will stick it in the hole if I can. These rebels are violating the Constitution in order to destroy the Union; I will violate the Constitution, if necessary, to save the Union; and I suspect, Chase, that our Constitution is going to have a rough time of it before we get done with this row."[21]

Note that Lincoln, a lawyer, did not argue that his idea was actually constitutional if seem from a different angle. He did not try to downplay the effect of his proposal. He acknowledged Chase's objections, and then went on to further clarify his position – to make his intentions known. All of this was related to a man, Secretary Chase, who could have been simply ordered to carry out the president's wishes.

Abraham Lincoln had sworn to uphold the Constitution and had spoken eloquently of its power and necessity. Here, he not only says he is willing to set it aside; he admits he is doing some violence to our founding ideals. Lincoln was adhering to his first purpose here: saving the Union. And he was respectful enough of Chase to be honest about his motivations.

Try and imagine a politician today being so nakedly honest. Every leader has to make wrenchingly difficult decisions. Being honest to others about how one's priorities play out is not just candid; it is respectful of the intelligence of others.

---

21. Phillips, *Lincoln on Leadership* 44

Probity is not just about honesty and trust; it is about respect. Scratch the surface of any one of these 10 leadership characteristics and we will find that most – or all – of the other characteristics are contained within. Probity demonstrates respect and a healthy dose of courage. Respect is an essential trait of the holistic thinker and the influencer (as opposed to the manipulator). Each characteristic is a piece of the mosaic that makes up the definition of every other characteristic.

I was raised in a religious tradition that emphasized the interconnectedness of morals and behaviors, so the fact that each characteristic contains elements of the others makes sense to me. In school and in church, we were taught to develop a conscience – to find a moral center from teachings and our own experience – and then to follow it. In seminary, where I studied for a while toward becoming a priest, I found that morals and principles were a source of strength in everyday behavior.

Let's not sugarcoat reality, though. Probity can be a source of strength, but it can also leave a leader feeling vulnerable and exposed. Probity can mean admitting when we are wrong, as Jim Treace would attest.

I have known Jim since the 1990s, when he and a venture capital firm bought the company where I worked, Xomed Surgical Products, Inc. But his story begins further back, in the 1980s when he was CEO of Concept, Inc.[22]

Jim had been recruited down to Concept on Florida's gulf coast to turn around a medical supply company. This was a publicly traded company that had not introduced any new products in seven years; it was treading water. Revenue was predominantly from low-margin items like penlights.[23] In short order, Jim had production working on new arthroscopy devices – for orthopedic surgeons to use repairing knee and other joint injuries – and was preparing a market launch. Looking at his sales team of 16 people scattered across the

22. A manufacturer of medical equipment, Concept is the company that became ConMed Linvatec Corp.
23. Small, battery-operated flashlights commonly used by optometrists and other doctors in patient examinations.

country, he paused. These were good people, but they did not have relationships with the orthopedic surgeons who would be buying the new devices. Meanwhile, Concept's stock price was getting hammered.

"I worried that I would not be able to get our new technology into the market with our all-employee sales team. I really needed a quick market punch," Jim said. "So I called our sales team into the office and told them that we were going to license the new product line to a non-employee, independent sales team.

"You should have seen their faces. I was making a business decision. But their faces looked like a football team that just heard they weren't even good enough to sit on the bench and should just turn in their jerseys.

"I walked out of there feeling like it was a bad decision. And it was not just about their faces. If I did this, I realized, I would be taking my number one product line and maybe getting a big bang on sales immediately, but in the long run? I would not be fostering a good employee-customer-shareholder relationship. I know that all three constituents must be served and I was leaving employees out."

Telling the truth to himself was, in some ways, easier than telling the truth to others. This is why Jim Treace commanded respect, though. Within a day, he called the outside sales group and told their representative that his company would not be getting the contract. "The guy threatened me, saying they would bury me in the marketplace," Jim remembers. "After that conversation, I knew I had done the right thing."

The next step was harder. Relationships and confidence needed to be repaired. The sales team had been undermined, and they would need a good dose of self-assurance to push into new territory. Jim flew to Chicago, Los Angeles, Dallas and Philadelphia to meet with his sales teams, admit that he had been wrong, and talk about how to get Concept's salespeople – as well as sales management – ready for the new product line.

Concept's leadership threw all necessary resources into the effort – coordinating meetings, getting introductions, conducting special training. Within three years, Concept was the market leader in arthroscopic devices, selling more in a day than its closest competitors sold in a month.

True honesty is not just for big decisions and emergency situations, however. Probity demands openness – ongoing communication with the entire organization. This is the most important path to trust.

People who work for us and with us need to know who we are and what we intend. Three important questions form a kind of hierarchy of trust in the minds of employees, according to Lou Holtz, respected head coach of the storied University of Norte Dame football team. Team members want to know: Do you care about me? Can I trust you? Are you committed to excellence?

Of these questions, I believe the second one is central to all relationships. According to a Harris Interactive Poll performed for Deloitte LLP's fourth annual Ethics and Workplace Survey in 2010, one third of 754 employed adults polled said they intended to look for another job in the coming year. Of that group, 48 percent said they hoped to leave because they had lost trust in their employer and 46 percent said a lack of transparent communication had led to that loss of trust.

There are many reasons to seek new employment. Money, family and geography all spring to mind as important motivators in leaving a job. But when nearly half of all employees who want to leave do so because of a lack of transparent communication led to a loss of faith, we know that probity is critical. Considering the cost of recruiting and training employees – to say nothing of the myriad costs associated with low performance from lack of commitment – honesty and trust become issues that are financial as well as emotional.

I do not mean to downplay the importance of the emotional environment in that last statement. Finances are important, but many of us have seen workplaces virtually implode around emotional issues, too. And the lack of probity is often at the root.

When I first arrived at Xomed as director of Operations for three plants – a few years before Jim Treace joined us – there were many signs of trouble. The lunchrooms were divided along racial lines. People complained about fairness – or its lack – and talked bitterly about people who were not doing their jobs, or who were not held accountable.

The executive offices, meanwhile, embraced a command-and-control leadership style that emphasized the numbers. People were pushed to "make the month" and cut costs without much regard to the bigger picture. Leadership wanted a continuous improvement initiative, but I discovered quickly that the company lacked both the discipline and trust necessary for a lean environment.

Anyone seeking cultural change needs a lever and the one I was given was not perfect: moving to a pay-for-performance system. Switching to new payment scheme can cause massive anxiety in a company, particularly where there are trust issues. But I seized on the change as an opportunity to talk to employees about what we meant by performance.

Those conversations, individually and in small groups, uncovered a lot of issues. Distrust was everywhere. We launched the *7 Habits* interpersonal training. We set goals for performance and started regular team huddles in the various departments to talk about how we were doing *as teams*. Once team members saw that there was no blame rolling downhill when we did not meet goals – that we worked on fixing processes instead of faulting people – trust began to build. We started talking about how to make production better and results soon followed.

This, I have found, is the operational benefit to open communication: If we listen to employees and then act on the information given, process improvements become a natural outgrowth of conversation.

Jim Treace found the same thing at Concept. Like a lot of chief executives, he announced that he had an open-door policy. But a passive policy either causes too many haphazard intrusions or no communication at all. So, Jim began inviting random employees to join small-group coffee klatches. The rule was that people could talk about anything on their minds during these meetings – family, work, whatever – and that nothing spoken would leave the room unless they agreed.

"I'll never forget one lady who told me during a coffee klatch that she was afraid she was going to lose her job. She had been with us something like 10 years and was a good employee," Jim remembered. "I asked her why, and she said she just wasn't able to do as much work as she used to."

The woman's job was testing circuitry as it came off the line. She picked a circuit, plugged it in, performed a test and moved on to the next. Only now, she was having a hard time getting the plugs to fit. Fiddling with the connection each and every time was slowing her down.

"After coffee, I followed her back out to the line and watched. Sure enough, the plugs weren't fitting right," Jim recalled. "I told her to stop the line. There was obviously a manufacturing defect with the plugs and if she – who knew the products so well and handled this connection dozens of times daily – was having a hard time getting the plugs to fit, imagine what was happening to our customers."

Of course, just because open communication is useful does not mean it will always be pretty or comfortable. Probity means being honest – as well as accepting the honesty that is thrust upon us. If we skip ahead a few years, my point will be clear.

By the end of the 1990s, Xomed was a different company. Jim Treace had joined us as CEO and brought in F. Barry Bays as COO. The change in ownership brought changed expectations and within weeks, the entire executive team – with the exception of me and one other manager – was fired. There were some rocky moments in the beginning. A few months into his tenure, Jim Treace discovered that the company's cash reserves were dangerously low and the following week's payroll and bills may not be covered.

Probity

Jim went back to Warburg Pincus seeking cash. Their answer: Warburg was a venture capital firm, not a bank. Jim quietly arranged with a local bank to have funds available, backed by his own finances. Xomed did not run out of cash, but it was close. Jim tried to keep it quiet, but we all found out soon enough. Jim used it as a teaching moment and told his officers, "One of my basic values is 'Don't run out of cash, no matter what.' Running out of cash hurts employees and you don't want to work for a company that treats people that way," Jim said.

Not long after that, I happened to be in a shop where our employees were forming PVC. I knew it from the smell. And I knew from earlier experience with this kind of manufacturing that I should not be able to smell that heated PVC. It was a sure sign that some toxic chemicals were off-gassing and endangering our workers. I immediately went to Jim and Barry Bays. I was a little nervous because I knew money was tight and I was about to tell them that we needed about $25,000 for a new ventilation system in that area. It would be a test of their integrity. "Is this the right thing to do?" Barry asked.

"It is," I answered. Jim said, "Never hesitate to do the right thing."

They did not ask for detailed measurements regarding levels of toxic outgassing. They did not ask if anyone complained. They said: Do the right thing, always.

After that, I felt like I was free to do what was right for Xomed and our employees. The lean initiative gathered momentum as everyone became engaged in turning that company around. Within three years, Medtronic purchased Xomed for 10 times the earlier sales price.[24]

While the lean initiative was making such great strides, our facility in Jacksonville won the Shingo Prize and we were named one of the "Top 10 Plants in America" by *IndustryWeek* magazine. It was a heady time. We had lots of

---

24. Warburg Pincus purchased Xomed in April 1996 for slightly less than $90 million. Medtronic acquired the company in 1999 for about $900 million.

groups coming in to tour our sites, to learn how we applied lean. I was asked to give talks around the country and happily accepted most of them.

I told myself that I was respecting my team by staying out of their way. That's not the way they saw it. A few of my team members commented on my frequent absences, but I brushed it off. Finally, my boss pointed out the ill effects of my missing-in-action status and I had to acknowledge I was not really serving my team. Finally, I admitted the truth: I liked traveling. I liked the attention. People asked for details of our success and were impressed. But impressing others was not really helping the lean effort at Medtronic.

Had I been more conscious of honesty – more inclined toward probity – I would have taken to heart what my team members were telling me. I would not have waited for my boss to pull me aside. This is a hard lesson I have learned over the years: The truth comes at a person from all sides – from below as well as above – and a good leader is open to hearing it, no matter the direction.

Learning to lead through trust and honesty, learning to hear the truth and act upon it, is a long road. There is more to learn every day.

So, why not take a short cut? Every leader knows that we can spark employees into action through manipulation or fear. But manipulation and fear are temporary motivators.

Probity and the trust it engenders in a workplace are sustainable motivators. People treated fairly, respectfully and honestly will give even more than what is asked. Becoming transparently honest is not easy, but it is the mark of great leadership. Probity creates trust and sustainable relationships – and that is what helps drives an organization to excellence.

Probity

Five Questions on Probity

1. Is there a bright line between truth and fiction, or have you allowed the line to blur?
2. What would your employees say about your level of honesty?
3. Does your team reliably know how you will react or what you will do in a given set of circumstances? Are you constant?
4. Are your team members honest?
5. How do you encourage a culture of probity?

INFLUENCE

Long before he delivered his "House Divided" speech or the historic "Gettysburg Address," Abraham Lincoln understood what it took to win over an audience. At 15, Lincoln was already repeating almost word for word sermons he had heard in church.[25] As a young lawyer traveling around the sparsely settled regions of Illinois, he honed his storytelling skills on the courthouse steps and in the local taverns.[26]

When he ran for the U.S. Senate against Stephen Douglas, he acknowledged that his skills were homespun, saying, "I am not a master of language; I have not a fine education; I am not capable of entering into a disquisition of dialectics, as you call it."[27] Lincoln's looks often worked against him. He was angular and given to thrusting his hands into his pockets before he spoke, and he had a high-pitched voice that could become shrill when he got excited.[28]

Historians believe Lincoln's power of persuasion lay in representing simple questions and answers that everyone could understand.[29] One example is the speech that catapulted Lincoln from the regional stage to the presidential spotlight on Feb. 27, 1860 at Cooper Union, a recently established college in New York.

Largely unknown in New York and stumping as a fledgling Republican Party candidate, Lincoln faced a crowd of fifteen hundred who had braved the fierce

---

25. David Hirsch and Dan Van Haften, *Abraham Lincoln and the Structure of Reason* (Savas Beatie, 2010) 4
26. Goodwin, *Team of Rivals.* 8
27. Hirsch and Van Haften, *Abraham Lincoln and the Structure of Reason.* 216
28. Phillips, *Lincoln on Leadership.* 146
29. Hirsch and Van Haften, *Abraham Lincoln and the Structure of Reason.* 46

cold and snow and paid twenty-five cents apiece to hear him speak.[30] Slavery was the topic on every mind and Lincoln focused his answer to his pro-slavery opponents on the belief that the founding fathers intended to restrict slavery in new territory. Lincoln asked: "Can we cast our votes with their view, and against our own? In view of our moral, social, and political responsibilities, can we do this? Wrong as we think slavery is, we can yet afford to let it alone where it is, because that much is due to the necessity arising from its actual presence in the nation; but can we, while our votes will prevent it, allow it to spread into the National Territories, and to overrun us here in these Free States? If our sense of duty forbids this, then let us stand by our duty, fearlessly and effectively."

The speech was nearly eight thousand words long and took Lincoln more than an hour to deliver – lengthy even by the standards of the day. But Lincoln's arguments and his ability to lead the audience through his reasoning stirred the crowd. Some cheered. One captivated eyewitness wrote, "his face lighted up as with an inward fire; the whole man was transfigured. I forgot his clothes, his personal appearance, and his individual peculiarities. Presently, forgetting myself, I was on my feet like the rest, yelling like a wild Indian, cheering this wonderful man."[31]

Even nineteenth-century journalist Horace Greeley was impressed. He wrote, "No man ever before made such an impression on his first appeal to a New-York audience."[32]

Lincoln surely had the gift of persuasion. But every leader who has tried to effect change in an organization knows that sometimes, persuasion is not enough. We can use all the fancy oratorical tricks in the book and push people in the direction we want them to go – for a while. Eventually though, people will revert to their natural inclinations, to the comfortable and familiar.

---

30. Phillips, *Lincoln on Leadership.* 147-148
31. Lincoln, Abraham. "Full Text. Abraham Lincoln Cooper Union Address." *The New York Times.* May 4, 2004. http://www.nytimes.com/2004/05/02/nyregion/03lincoln-text.html?pagewanted=all
32. Times Topics. Horace Greeley. *The New York Times.* http://topics.nytimes.com/top/reference/timestopics/people/g/horace_greeley/index.html

To effect real, lasting change requires more subtlety and time – it needs influence. Influence means guiding people to finding the right answers on their own, so that the right path becomes their natural inclination. The line between persuasion and influence can seem blurred. But for me, persuasion means nudging people toward the finish line; influence is helping people discover the finish line on their own.

Whether Lincoln would have agreed with my definitions is hard to say. But he certainly employed both persuasion and influence strategically. When hoping to win over large crowds, he used persuasive arguments and elegant language. In closer quarters, when dealing with his sometimes adversarial cabinet members, he spent time in their homes, asking their opinions, discussing current events, and telling his gently pointed stories. In memoirs and letters, Lincoln's team members recalled those meetings in detail. There were no speeches, no power plays; there was a lot of listening and idea sharing. In this way, through the gentler art of influence, Lincoln's fiercest critics became his allies.

All of us are subjected to the power of influence from a very young age. We watch our parents and teachers and take lessons from their behavior. Some of my own earliest memories continue to have influence on my daily behavior – and not just because many of those memories took place in any child's dream factory.

My father, Gerry Bussell, managed a candy factory. Part of the Great Atlantic and Pacific Tea Co., my dad's candy factory in Brooklyn, New York, was straight out of an episode of "I Love Lucy." Conveyers took candies to people who would assemble them into boxed assortments and around any corner, it seemed, Lucille Ball and Ethel Mertz could have been stuffing their mouths with chocolates to hide their inability to keep up with the line. My brothers and I loved visiting the plant with Dad on the weekends because we could always snag a handful of candy while he checked in on production issues. In later years, my brothers and I worked in the plant on summers and school holidays, shoveling sugar and loading supplies and learned how physically demanding that work could be. Candy held less interest to us than the three or four sandwiches that my mom would pack each of us for lunch.

Influence

What I really remember of the candy factory, though, is riding on my father's shoulders as he strode through the plant he managed, talking to me about how things were made. Dad would tell me about the machines and what they did, but he really talked about the people behind the mechanisms. He would tell me what a candy sorter did, but always follow it up with something like, "Joe runs the candy sorter most days. He's been working here for 15 years and he really knows this machine inside and out."

Looking down from the great height of my dad's shoulders, I learned that production lines were not gears and belts so much as they were people. He told me, "Treat people how they want to be treated, not how you want to treat them."

In school, I studied philosophy and theology. When it came time to get a job, however, I pursued manufacturing. And in every job I had, I thought about how people wanted to be treated, because of Dad's early influence.

Every person in a leadership position – whether a CEO or a first-time kaizen team leader – is constantly influencing the actions and reactions of everyone in his or her orbit, for good or ill. Associates are always watching us, looking for signs of the "real" meaning behind our words and our true intentions. Much of the time, we blind ourselves to that unspoken influence we have. We choose to forget the old adage, *actions speak louder than words*, in the hope that we can simply tell people what we want and how everyone should act. "Telling," after all, is so much simpler than "living" out our own directives. But think back on bad leaders encountered – just about everyone has known one – and there is a good chance that they share this trait of "telling" instead of "living."

A senior vice president that I worked for early in my career, for instance, was a vocal proponent of inclusive strategic planning sessions. Once or twice a year, he would pull his planning, engineering, and supply chain managers, plus his plant directors, into a two-day meeting to consider objectives and goals for the year. All of us would diligently prepare for these meetings, gathering figures, considering options – trying to bring our best game to the table.

Our leader began the meeting telling us his ideas, then asked for reactions. In the beginning, we would have rigorous discussions. But after a time it became clear that the goals and objectives we left with were always the goals and objectives our leader stated in the beginning. Over time, disagreements ceased. Discussion became flat. We could have doodled through those meetings and we all knew it, so we brought less and less to the table. What was the point? The leader obviously did not want our input.

Now, let's make a 180-degree turn to F. Barry Bays. Brought in as Xomed's chief operating officer by Jim Treace after Warburg Pincus bought the company, Barry needed to take charge and turn around operations. Before I met him, I was waiting for a whole new set of marching orders from a stranger.

When Barry and I first met, however, I do not recall a single decree. Instead, we walked out onto the factory floor and spent about five hours there. He asked questions – of me, of engineers and operators, of everyone. These were not shotgun questions; it was clear he was not trying to trip people up. It did not matter whether he was talking to an executive or someone sweeping the floor, Barry treated people respectfully and always, it seemed, he had more questions.

Over the next few years, I had several mini-coaching sessions with Barry every week. When I had a problem or I was unsure about direction, he had a willing ear. Barry would hear me out and then ask a few questions. I would always leave those sessions with a workable plan – or at least, a clear idea of the extra information I needed before I could make a plan. Barry never gave me the plan, however. I left those sessions knowing that *I* made the plan.

Only later did I realize how much I learned from Barry – the man who would not tell me anything. I learned that leading by example is the shortest route to influencing behavior, and that asking questions is not a sign of weakness. Questions, in fact, can be a way to confer power to others. Barry's questions always led me to focus, to identify the most important expectations, and to deliver on those first. Barry Bays gave me the freedom to lead, with the assurance of his safety net, and gave me – through influence alone – the most important tool in my leadership bucket: Socratic questioning.

Credited as a founder of Western philosophy, Socrates and his style of questioning is known to us mostly through the work of Plato and his dialogues.[33]
In these dialogues, would-be students approached Socrates with questions
of morality and ethics, seeking wisdom, and Socrates probed deeper into the
questions. Socrates asked about assumptions, facts and word definitions, and
led his questioner away from superficial answers. Socrates' questions encouraged his audience to consider the problem from many angles, and to provide
their own answers.

Put to death by hemlock poisoning after being judged an atheist by the government of Athens in 469 BC, Socrates did not leave behind a written record.
What we know of his philosophy, we surmise from the questions he asked and
the very fact that he asked questions instead of pontificating. Asking questions
is an act of humility. When we ask questions, we invite others to share their
knowledge and experience, and admit that we do not know all.

In a lean environment, Socratic questioning is not so different from the Five
Whys. In each case, we ask successive questions in order to drive deeper into
the heart of the matter, or the root cause. And since the time of Barry Bays,
I have found those questions to be an essential part of coaching – which, in
many ways, is simply an on-going exercise in influence and reciprocal learning.

Coaching requires a good deal of patience. It is part of human nature to want
to reach the goal, to push people or things to the conclusion we have in mind.
The best coaching moments I have experienced, however, involved people
who ended up in an entirely different place than I predicted. Invariably, I
learned a lot from these incidents. Each time, I became more committed to the
Socratic process – for the joy of learning a new way of thinking, and a fresh
point of view.

People that are being coached can also experience that joy of discovery, but

---

33. While Plato was chiefly a fiction writer and not a historian, the dialogues are useful for
showing Socrates in action, from a student who was present for many such sessions.

only if we let them. If we poke and prod with our questions, obviously pushing toward a particular conclusion, people just end up feeling manipulated. There's no joy in that. I like to imagine good coaching as leading a person into a new landscape. If we tell a person to walk over the hill in order to see the ocean with a big rock and sea lions lazing around in the sun and salt spray, the view is undermined by our conclusions. But if we tell that person to simply walk over the hill and report back, the person being coached takes in the experience with fresh eyes, and maybe we learn that there is a cove in the rock we never noticed.

This kind of coaching acknowledges the power of different points of view, and respects the strengths that others bring to the table. Strong leaders know that the last thing they want around the table is a bunch of clones. Done right, this coaching also helps to reveal people who are intractable.

For many years, I was under the impression that I could use influence and coaching to rehabilitate anyone – that all could discover the true meaning of words like lean and team. Still, I encountered people who seemed driven to undermine fellow team members and lean efforts. I worked hard at coaching, and some situations dragged on far too long. To let backstabbing fester, I discovered, is to influence an entire organization in a negative direction. Barry had a favorite saying that "leopards don't change their spots." He was right. Acknowledging that people are fundamentally unique – non-clones – means that we also have to recognize when a person will not be influenced or persuaded to truly join the team. Coaching means really getting to know the person being coached, as well as guiding.

"Every single day I have to work at being a coach," said Karl Wadensten, president of VIBCO Vibrators, Inc. "In Eastern cultures, people are trained to observe, to use the Socratic method, and to guide. In this country, we're raised to lead and control. And nobody just changes overnight."

I have known Karl for a number of years and I am still surprised if I see him sitting down. Filled with kinetic energy, Karl has a big voice, likes bright colors, and was definitely raised in the Western leadership style. His father started

Influence

VIBCO in 1962, making the kind of huge industrial vibrators and shaking tables used for everything from packaging and conveyor belts to moving and forming concrete. Knowing that Karl would succeed him some day, Karl's dad handpicked Karl's college courses, all the way through his graduate degree. Karl was groomed to be the kind of command-and-control leader that most business schools were producing in those days. But it never sat easily with him.

In the mid 1990s, Karl discovered the Young Presidents' Organization and a completely different way of thinking about leadership. "I found people who were facing the same problems as me, who had been in my shoes, and would talk openly about real issues. They talked about feelings, emotions. Business people! I learned to suspend judgment. There were no 'should haves' or quick fix-it advice."

Founded in 1950, the YPO has a single mission: better leaders through the exchange of information and ideas. With about 20,000 members in 110 countries around the world, the YPO would have the world's third largest GDP if the members all combined their companies. It was here that Karl learned that he had to find, to clarify, his own meaning before he could impart that to others.

"I learned to ask questions and to use more 'I' statements," Karl said. "If I saw a bunch of work piled up at someone's station, for instance, I stopped saying, 'What the hell is going on here?' I started saying, 'I'm feeling stressed out because I don't know what's happening. Can you help me gain some clarity?'"

So, Karl was already looking for a different style of leadership – a different way of doing business – in 2002 when the realization that he and VIBCO needed to change hit him full force. It started with a good thing: an order for $20,000 worth of vibrators for an important bridge project. It was cause for celebration.

The deadline for those vibrators to be shipped came and went. Missing a delivery date was a common enough occurrence that Karl was not even notified. The second delivery date came and went without a shipment, too.

"A week later, the third promised delivery date, our distributor calls and he's crying. A grown man, crying," Karl recalled, "He's got $10 million in contracts on this bridge and he might lose the whole thing because we didn't keep our promises. People could lose jobs. Our distributor is afraid of losing everything, so he's crying."

In bed with a case of bronchitis when he got the call, Karl immediately got up and went to the shop. He put on a welding coat, gathered his people and got those vibrators built and shipped. When they were done, there should have been a celebration, but he did not feel like cheering.

"I just felt like I didn't want to work for this organization. I value my word to people – to employees, customers, distributors – and we couldn't keep it," Karl said. "If I was feeling that way, as president, how the heck were they feeling? They don't have the power to change it. I do."

VIBCO began a lean journey with a "true north" statement born of that moment: "Same Day, Next Day." Karl drew a factory leading to a truck leading to another factory. He labeled the first building VIBCO and "today," the truck was labeled "tomorrow," the customer's factory was labeled "next day." The goal was to get every order shipped on the same day or, at least, the next business day. To remind everyone of the consequences, he included a frowning, sobbing face on the drawing. It was that drawing, reproduced often, that helped everyone understand not just the idea, but the emotion and energy of VIBCO's true north. It was the new expectation.

Using 5S, SMED[34] and redesigning workflow, product started moving faster and more reliably. But it was cross-training VIBCO's 100 employees into multiple jobs and work areas that effected the biggest changes at VIBCO.

People who worked in the offices became reliable team members on the shop floor, when needed. Welders also became teachers; assemblers took roles in the machine shop. People stepped out of comfort zones everywhere and found their fellow associates waiting for them, willing to train, to listen and to

---

34. SMED: single-minute exchange of die, or drastically reducing set-up time on machines.

simplify when confusion arose. This led to *Poka-yoke* – Japanese for "mistake-proofing" – and better standard work.

To allow everyone to be a teacher, Karl needed to step back, stop micro-managing, and encourage people to make independent decisions. He learned to influence instead of control. It was a Herculean effort, Karl said, but the company can now ship orders on the same day or the next business day 99 percent of the time – even though the company has expanded its product lines and offers more variation. VIBCO kaizen teams have reduced inventory by $2 million, improved quality by 85 percent and now turn their work-in-progress (WIP) inventory 88 times per year.

Karl's enthusiasm for lean overflowed. He talked about what his people were accomplishing at meetings of the Young Presidents' Organizations and with other leaders in his home state of Rhode Island. Karl saw businesses suffering in the recession and he knew lean could help. If everyone began improving with lean principles, all boats could rise. Rhode Island could be different. He vowed to begin by influencing other leaders.

VIBCO began hosting a Presidents' Event with a dozen leaders in attendance for a full day of tours and workshops. It became a monthly event that doubled in size each time until it grew, Karl said, into an avalanche. Presidents flew in from across the country and from as far away as New Zealand. People came by the busload. Rhode Island's governor came and then sent mayors, the general treasurer, and other state department heads to VIBCO to learn how to change mindsets.

Soon it became clear that what everyone was really studying were the people of VIBCO. The plant's cleanliness, machine layout and workflow were great, but it was the people – enthusiastic, knowledgeable and engaged – that everyone wanted to replicate.

"I'm a fanatic and a zealot for lean, and for the people that work for me," Karl said. "They do the impossible every day. It is not always pretty. It isn't a bunch of roses. But they are amazing and they know that I will break down barriers to make it happen for them. They come up with ideas; I help them make it happen. We feed each other. I just want to keep it going.

"What I keep telling other leaders, though, is that they have the same possibility in their companies. They just haven't tapped into the genius of their people."

Seeking an even wider audience for his lean message, Karl began a daily, hour-long show on an ABC Citadel radio station for about 18 months. Five days a week, he talked about lean from the mobile radio station in his office – or on the road, from hotels – and could claim 45,000 listeners. Now a two-hour show once a week, "Lean Nation" is the second most popular podcast download for the all-talk AM station. Hundreds of businesses have begun, resumed, or been supported in on-going lean journeys because of Karl's influence.

Still, Karl is always working on his own growth, on coaching and sharing instead of instructing and ordering. Sometimes, he even says those gut-wrenching three words, "I don't know." This quality of openness is probably what helped Karl see what few leaders would care to admit: the sometimes-disruptive nature of influence.

The influence that comes with the title "leader" is outsized. And we all enjoy the perks. When a leader needs information, a willing ear, a cup of coffee, there is almost always someone nearby ready to jump to the task. That associate does not mind being interrupted, really. It is for the boss.

"Most leaders have a gazillion balls in the air at all times. How we keep it all straight, or most of it, is to check on things as they occur to us. So, we're always asking people as we walk past, 'Hey, how's that project or problem going?' If the person doesn't have a ready answer, he or she will go get it. And now that one project or problem has undue precedence because the boss asked," Karl said.

Karl had to admit that he did not know how to delegate in a thoughtful way. So a kaizen team attacked the issue and came up with an interesting fix: the

Influence

Karl Needs Your Help Process Sheet. On a single sheet of paper, Karl now writes down his request and, more importantly, puts it into context and attaches a deadline. After stating the request, there are checkboxes for how the information should be delivered – via email, in person, etc. – and then the urgency. Checkboxes for urgency include:

- Please drop what you're doing and help right now!
- Today
- Within a week
- Within a month
- I will need this information in future. Fit it in where you can, but don't lose sight, because I'm going to ask you about it down the road.

In my mind, this worksheet reveals at least two of the essential characteristics of a lean leader, because it acknowledges Karl's influence while respecting the associate's time and workflow. It cannot be easy to stop and fill out a sheet of paper instead of simply asking for information in passing. Karl does it because he is committed to being a better leader, to putting his needs in context while giving employees the opportunity to get clarification and definitions.

Over the years, I have noticed that all leaders who seek to improve their own skills gravitate toward using influence instead of force. They display humility. They ask questions. They do not take advantage of the others in a weaker position.

This requires a particular kind of strength in a person – a strength I have seen more often from lean practitioners than traditional leaders. In fact, I was introduced to this style of leadership early on by watching John Shook.

Now, in my lean novice years, I was in awe of John Shook. A former employee of Toyota in Japan, John helped bring Toyota's production, engineering, and management systems to the U.S. when opening the NUMMI plant in California. In later years, he helped Toyota spread its systems around the world in other plants and became one of the most influential and enthusiastic lean leaders.[35] John's talks on leadership were so inspiring, I would attend any conference where he was speaking, just to learn a little more. I was practically stalking John until the day he agreed to come to Xomed's Jacksonville, Florida, plant to see what we were doing.

A gemba walk with a master, as most lean leaders know, is a nerve-wracking experience. I wanted my team's efforts to shine, to be praised, but I also wanted to see flaws or opportunities through the fresh eyes of the master. I waited for judgment.

Like Barry Bays, though, John Shook only had questions. There were no pronouncements about the fitness of our lean efforts. John asked questions, and by the questions he asked – of operators, engineers and executives – we learned to see through his eyes. We learned to ask our own questions, to study systems the way he did, and the Xomed team learned to trust in our own ability to come up with good answers.

A leader like John Shook – or Barry Bays or Karl Wadensten or anyone, really, who dares to take a position out front – has a certain amount of influence already implied by his or her position. Think of it as the green jacket from the Masters Tournament. When a leader is chosen, he or she dons the jacket and even if nobody talks about the jacket, everyone knows who is wearing it. We watch the person in the jacket, taking tips from their behavior, because on some level, everyone wants to wear the green jacket.

The question is whether that influence is squandered, or if it is used to empower the people who follow.

---

35. John Shook took over leadership of the Lean Enterprise Institute in 2011, upon the retirement of founder James Womack.

Five Questions for Influence

1. What is the most mission-critical behavior you want from your team and how do you model that?
2. How do you recognize your own influence and control its impact?
3. Are you a coach or an instructor? What would your direct reports call you?
4. When was the last time you were surprised by the way in which someone in your organization solved a problem?
5. When was the last time you tried to persuade a person to act? How might you use influence instead?

CONTINUOUS LEARNER

It was the early 1980s, about five years in to a civil war that was tearing his country apart, when Sami Bahri arrived for a meeting at the university in Beirut. He thought he was there to volunteer his services at a dental clinic. No, the department chair told him; the professor who taught prosthodontics had fled the country. Could Dr. Bahri teach his courses?

Dr. Bahri studied the textbooks over the weekend and dove in. A few years later, while the country suffered political fracturing, betrayals and bloody street wars, the university lost its government support and accreditation. A new dental school was launched at Université Libanaise and Dr. Bahri was selected its first director. With a team of dentists who were enthusiastic but untrained as teachers, Dr. Bahri set out to study education.

The dentists traveled to Los Angeles, Florida, Switzerland, France and Germany, seeking guidance in how best to train the next generation of dentists and set up the necessary clinics. Back in Beirut, the team met every Monday to discuss best teaching methods for hours on end, through countless dinners and late nights. So, when the dental school and clinics were up and running, Dr. Bahri was sure the system was based on sound principles.

That is why, two years later, this thought was so puzzling to him. He was standing in the middle of the dental school's 60-chair clinic, watching the hive of activity. With dental chairs separated only by half walls, he could see everything: the patients receiving cleanings, gum treatments, crowns and fillings. He noticed that many of the patients' faces were familiar. People typically came back several times in order to get all the work done, he realized.

"Standing there, I had the idea that maybe it would be better to treat one patient at a time. Instead of treating them as separate procedures – a filling, a cleaning, a crown – maybe we should be treating the patient, all at once," Dr. Bahri said.

"I thought about how we might do it. I started to see it, and there were so many variables. It was mind-boggling. Then I dismissed the idea. Dental schools have been around for a long time, I thought. People must have surely tried this and failed."

It was a moment that many of us have experienced – a glimpse into another way of working; a simple, revolutionary idea – that we dismiss with the thought: "There must be a reason why people don't do it that way."

Fast-forward a few years. Dr. Bahri left his beloved, war-torn country and moved to Florida. He opened an office in Jacksonville and developed a habit of listening to audiobooks during his daily commute or whenever he was in the car. He rented books on tape about language, etiquette, effective communication and regional histories.

The quintessential continuous learner, Dr. Bahri studied everything that could help him assimilate and build a practice. But the business of running an efficient medical office was still a mystery. After all the seminars and books about dentistry management systems, he was frustrated. He worked very fast, but patients typically waited two hours in his waiting room to see him. He had plenty of assistants, but even his assistants were waiting on him much of the time. He knew he was missing some key idea or ingredient.[36]

Through a friend, Dr. Michael Dagher, who was running a large emergency room in Jacksonville, Dr. Bahri discovered Total Quality Management (TQM). Dr. Dagher explained the ideas of W. Edwards Deming and how he was using manufacturing techniques to improve flow in his hospital. On his home computer, Dr. Dagher showed Dr. Bahri a dashboard with constantly updated key

36. Full disclosure: Dr. Bahri was my family dentist during this time and I was impressed with the quality of his work. But I stopped seeing him because I just could not take off an entire afternoon, waiting in his office.

performance indicators from the emergency room.

Galvanized, Dr. Bahri threw himself into TQM, but only achieved marginal improvements. Maybe a crown or a filling would be accomplished a little quicker, but people were still waiting. And Dr. Bahri was still working as fast as he could – through every lunch and late into the evening – without much relief.

One evening, driving home after another frustrating day, Dr. Bahri found himself listening to Jim Womack as he described watching children folding, stapling and stamping newsletters at a kitchen table. Dr. Bahri pulled abruptly to the side of the road. In that simple description of one-piece flow from *Lean Thinking*,[37] Dr. Bahri briefly glimpsed again that 60-chair clinic in Lebanon and the idea he had for one-patient flow. It was not a complete vision; the full idea would take additional years and many more books to work out, but it was tantalizing.

Dr. Bahri got the book *Lean Thinking* and then flipped to the bibliography and started reading his way through that list too. He read books by Taiichi Ohno and Shigeo Shingo – both of whom helped create the Toyota Production System – and started experiments in his office.

"I did not really think I was implementing lean," Dr. Bahri said. "I was just excited about the things I was learning and would find someone on my staff willing to listen and we would just try it."

That statement is the best illustration of a continuous learner that I can imagine. Excited about what he was learning, Dr. Bahri looked for way to make it come to life. He gathered knowledge and took action. The best illustration of a *lean* continuous learner? He engaged whatever staff members he could, taught them what he had learned and then set about experimenting with improvements. He just did it.

---

37. James P. Womack and Donald T. Jones, *Lean Thinking: Banish Waste and Create Wealth in Your Corporation* (Simon and Schuster, 1996)

Continuous Learner

With so many health care organizations now investigating or implementing lean, it may no longer seem remarkable what Dr. Bahri did. But this was the late 1990s and early 2000s when Dr. Bahri was thinking about how to translate Shingo's teachings regarding single-minute exchange of die, SMED, to dentistry. It was a time when the division between front and back offices was absolute in most medical practices, and Dr. Bahri started cross-training.

"Our biggest functional breakthrough was realizing that SMED referred to the setup in a room," Dr. Bahri said. "With every new patient, we need to have a fresh set of sterilized tools and equipment that is specific to the patient needs. We worked on reducing the setup time for patients, and making sure that setup happened before we got there. When we did that, I was suddenly finished with patients in 20 minutes instead of an hour.

"I was done so fast, that I could ask patient if they wanted the next thing done – a filling or preparation for a crown maybe – right away instead of having to come back. That's when I started to see the way we would get to one-patient flow. Now, we identify patient appointments by value stream."

Dr. Bahri used lean principles to in-source much of the work that dentists send out, such as making crowns and bridges. Doctors in the Bahri Dental Group can diagnose the need, make a crown and install it all in a single appointment. With three additional dentists and an orthodontist – his brother, Gaby Bahri – now on staff, Bahri Dental Group patients are seen immediately 90 percent of the time. And Dr. Bahri often has time for a relaxed lunch with his brother at his favorite Lebanese restaurant.

At a Shingo Conference in 2007, Dr. Bahri presented his work and was named by Utah State University to be the world's "First Lean Dentist." Dr. Bahri's book, *Follow The Learner,* was published in 2009. [38]

Sami Bahri is a natural learner. I am not. Dr. Bahri's reflex is to constantly gather and synthesize more information; he does not go to sleep at night

---

38. Sami Bahri, *Follow the Learner: The Role of a Leader in Creating a Lean Culture* (Lean Enterprise Institute, 2009)

until he identifies at least one new thing he has learned that day to help him improve. I can only imagine being that diligent. While I cannot overemphasize the importance of being a continuous learner, for me – like for many others – it requires effort. And a good bit of courage, too.

Here is one of the stand-out memories from my postgraduate work: standing on my driveway in Waco, Texas, calmly explaining to my wife how I had decided not to start classes at Baylor University toward an MBA that day because, well, she needed me. Mary just looked at me.

We had just moved to Waco along with about 30 other Allergan, Inc. employees to set up a new business and I was in charge. Our children were quite small. I was already absorbed with my job, I told Mary. If I were studying for an MBA as well, I would not be much help for her. She just sighed and told me to go to school. Do it now, she said, or I would just keep thinking of new reasons not to.

The truth was, as Mary knew, I was over 40 and had not been in a university classroom in two decades. I had been an average student. Some anxiety around taking tests meant that my papers were often soaked with sweat and a little crumpled by the time I finished. I loved the kind of hands-on learning I had been doing in manufacturing. I excelled in environments where I could see the real-world effects of applied theories. Classrooms were another matter.

I will always be grateful that Mary gently pushed me off to school that morning, and my future employers should have thanked her, too. It was at Baylor that I discovered Stephen Covey, learned to work more effectively in teams, learned the essential ideas behind lean and the Toyota Production System, and discovered that learning in a classroom could be (almost) as enjoyable as learning how things worked in the real world. The trick, I discovered, was in applying what we learned as soon as possible and teaching it to others.

For me, continuous learning goes hand-in-glove with teaching. To really learn anything, I found that I needed to inhabit both ends of the education continuum – to be an absolute novice and a teacher at the same time.

In my early days at Kraft Foods, Inc. where my career began, and then at a start-up contact lens manufacturer called Hydron, I was thrown into numerous situations where I was both novice and boss. If I did not know anything about sales, for instance, it was a pretty sure bet someone was about to put me in charge of that – or customer service, or IT, or systems operations. The only way I survived was by keeping my eyes and ears open and learning everything I could.

As I got the opportunity to learn new subjects and methods – about teamwork or leadership or continuous improvement – I always made it a point to teach the new material to my team and then have them turn and teach it to their teams.

After reading the book *Lincoln on Leadership*, for instance, I shared it with my team and had each of them choose a topic and prepare a 15-minute report on how Lincoln might have handled a situation. The acts of preparing those presentations made each of us think more deeply about the life and leadership example of Lincoln. We absorbed more information by teaching. It was the kind of thing, I like to imagine, that Lincoln might have done.

Abraham Lincoln loved to read and, throughout his life, he devoured almost anything he could find: newspapers, poetry, legal books, books on Euclidean geometry and novels. It was this lifelong devotion to reading that served him well as a state representative. When Lincoln was only 25 years old, he decided to study law. He began by borrowing legal books from his friend John Stuart, and studied them until he could interpret legal documents on his own. Lincoln had a habit of taking his law books out into the woods and sprawling out on the ground to read them.[39] His answer for mastering a subject was easy: "Get the books, and read and study them," Lincoln told a law student in 1855.

During his nights off from traveling around the state as a circuit lawyer, Lincoln taught himself geometry, working out geometric equations he had gleaned from reading books written by the Greek mathematician Euclid.[40] Later, he

---

39 Goodwin, *Team of Rivals*. 54-55
40. Goodwin, *Team of Rivals*. 152

would spend hundreds of hours in the state library in Illinois preparing for his first anti-slavery speech in October 1854 at a state fair. He researched the Kansas-Nebraska Act so that he could write a clear and compelling rebuttal to his opponent Stephen Douglas. Lincoln called himself a slow learner, but he used his difficulty, he explained later, as an asset.

"I am slow to learn and slow to forget that which I have learned," Lincoln said. "My mind is like a piece of steel, very hard to scratch anything on it and almost impossible after you get it there to rub it out."[41] That state fair speech was the largest audience Lincoln had faced in his political career to date and when he finished, the audience broke into deafening applause.

One of Lincoln's strengths was his ability to acknowledge his limits, and to recognize where he needed to learn more. An early example was the 1855 patent infringement case, McCormick v. Manny. The McCormick Harvesting Machine Co. and the J.H. Manny Co. were fierce competitors in the new field of mechanical reaping. At the 1855 Paris Exposition, the two reapers were exhibited and the Manny Reaper was judged the winner. McCormick sued for patent infringement, launching one of the first U.S. cases involving intellectual property.

The Manny Company hired patent authority George Harding of Philadelphia as its lead attorney and a lesser-known litigator, Abraham Lincoln, because of Lincoln's proximity to the Northern District Court in Springfield, Illinois. But after the trial was moved to Cincinnati, Lincoln was benched and Harding hired a more experienced trial attorney, Edwin M. Stanton. Unfortunately, no one told Lincoln, who thought he was still arguing the case in court. Lincoln visited Manny's plant in Rockford, Illinois, to study the machine, piecing together a brief that he thought would be presented to the trial judge. Lincoln continued to research the case even as Manny's lead attorneys snubbed him, ignoring his letters and requests for information.

On the day of the trial, Lincoln met Stanton on his way to the courtroom, and

---

41. Goodwin, *Team of Rivals.* 164-169 Quoting from the Illinois State Register and David Herbert Donald, *Lincoln* (Simon & Schuster, 1995) 174

his hillbilly twang and overcoat stained at the armpits left an impression with Stanton: utter horror. Stanton pulled another attorney aside and said, "Why did you bring that d------d Ape here ... he does not know any thing and can do you no good." Stanton then turned on his heels and left. Throughout the trial, he continued to disregard Lincoln, even though all of Manny's lead attorneys stayed at the same hotel.[42]

Stanton's memories of Lincoln during that time remained strong, even after the trial. Later, he remarked, "I said that if that giraffe appeared on the case, I will throw up in my brief and leave."[43]

Though not welcome at the defense table, Lincoln stayed in the courtroom to observe the proceedings, studying Stanton's presentation and soaking in his complex arguments. Public humiliation did not deter Lincoln from acknowledging Stanton's superior courtroom skills and polish. When Lincoln became president, Stanton was one of his first cabinet appointments.

"It would have been a great mistake if I had spoken on this case; I did not fully understand it," Lincoln admitted later to a friend. But knowing Stanton had outclassed him in court did not make Lincoln resentful. In fact, he was impressed by his legal expertise and resolved to hit his law books again.

By the time he assumed the presidency in 1860, Lincoln had never served as a governor, a CEO or a military strategist. Everything was learned on the job. When it came to military strategy Lincoln was a novice, especially in contrast to Jefferson Davis, a Confederate general who was educated at the U.S. Military Academy at West Point.

"Did you know I am a military hero?" Lincoln joked once about his 80-day stint as a soldier during the Black Hawk War.[44] "I fought, bled, and came away

42. Goodwin, *Team of Rivals.* 174-175
43. Richard Lawrence Miller, *Lincoln and His World: The Path to the Presidency, 1854-1860* (McFarland, 2012) 98-101
44.Wilmer T. Jones, *Generals in Blue and Gray* (Praeger Publishers, 2004) 4

[after] charges upon the wild onions" and "a good many bloody struggles with the Musquetoes."[45]

Lincoln clashed with many of the generals who served early in his administration, so when it came to mastering his role as commander in chief, he took his own advice to study the books.[46] He borrowed the *Elements of Military Art and Science,* General Henry Halleck's treatises on military strategy, from the Library of Congress and recorded them to memory as he had the Kansas-Nebraska Act years earlier.[4748]

Lincoln "gave himself, night and day, to the study of the military situation," his private secretary John Hay wrote later. "He read a large number of strategical works. He pored over the reports from the various departments and districts of the field of war."[49]

By soaking up what military historians and strategists had to offer, Lincoln acted as a de facto commander until he found generals who could carry out his strategies – namely, engaging the Confederate Army in battle.

Imagine that for a moment: being commander in chief in wartime, admitting that you know little of war craft beyond the fact that your generals should engage the enemy, and then learning everything you can on the subject, quickly.

We have all met people who seem to believe that admitting lack of knowledge is a weakness. This type of person pretends to know the answer. Favorite expression: "been there, done that." This urge to pretend knowledge inevitably leads to lack of observation. The pretender covers up valuable information or looks the other way, for fear of showing limitations. Another variation on

45. Eric Foner, *Our Lincoln: New Perspectives on Lincoln and His World* (W.W. Norton & Co., 2009) 19
46. Wilmer T. Jones, *Generals in Blue and Gray* 11
47. William K. Klingaman, *Abraham Lincoln and the Road to Emancipation, 1861-1865* (Viking Penguin, 2002)
48. Goodwin, *Team of Rivals.* 426
49. James M. McPherson, *Tried by War: Abraham Lincoln As Commander in Chief* (Penguin Press, 2008) 3

this theme are the executives who suffer from arrested development – having learned "everything" in the first 15 years of a career, they keep applying it over and over, no matter the consequences.

Had Lincoln been a pretender instead of a learner, I might have needed a passport to leave Florida today.

Continuous learning forces us out of comfortable routines; it never allows us to rest on past laurels, because there is always something new to discover. The continuous learner knows that to stop learning means to halt growth; the learner is always looking for new approaches.

Like the influencer, who uses Socratic questions to guide people deeper into the questions, the continuous learner asks questions and relies on observation to hone his or her understanding of the issues. A problem well-defined, I have learned, is a problem half-solved.

The importance of defining the question or problem was brought home to me by John Shook, especially. While going on a gemba walk through a Medtronic plant one day, he asked to see an A3. I had to admit that I did not know what an A3 was. With characteristic patience, John explained the method of using a single sheet of paper to describe a problem, the proposed solution, the steps to take to implement that solution and, if successful, the steps needed to make it standard work.

After John left that day, I found there was more than one way to work an A3 and that advocates on either side could feel pretty passionate about their choice. Some people used the DMAIC cycle, which stands for define, measure, analyze, improve, control. Others use PDCA – plan, do, check, act – popularized by W. Edwards Deming, to organize the work of the A3. To me, these seemed to be equally useful methods for helping people work through problems using the scientific method. It was the discipline of putting the question, solution, required action and outcome on a single sheet of paper, I decided, that was far more important than the acronym we used to organize the work. What mattered is that the people on the line understood and used this tool.

So we put out a survey, asking folks which acronym made sense to them. The people chose DMAIC and that is what we used.

Learning should, whenever possible, be fun. It should actually make people feel better about themselves, their jobs and their colleagues. The atmosphere most damaging to continuous learning is a blame culture, where people are singled out or ridiculed for mistakes and missteps, where people are told that it is wrong to try new methods (if they do not work) and ideas.

Learning requires that we stick our necks out a little, that we assume the mindset of the novice – even as we lead others – and go fearlessly into the unknown.

Five Questions on Continuous Learning

1. When was the last time you said, "I don't know?"
2. Would your subordinate be comfortable knowing that you overheard him or her saying, "I don't know?" What would they assume your reaction would be?
3. When was the last time you got excited about an idea?
4. Is there time for teaching or coaching in your schedule, and in your team's schedules?
5. Would you congratulate a team member for bringing in an idea you had not heard of or considered?

PERSISTENCE

A lot of parents think of their children as extraordinary. My son really was. Complications during childbirth left him with serious challenges during his formative years. His cognitive skills were great, but the muscles that help us form words were underdeveloped in him and required three years of speech therapy. In fact, all his motor skills needed work. He had no strength in his hands and when he finally began walking, one leg always was lagging behind. Born into a family of athletes, he did not learn how to throw a ball until he was nearly eight.

But here is the marvel of James: he studied everyone else's movement, repeated actions over and over trying to gain through repetition what came naturally to people like me. For hours, he would work with me at throwing a ball and then "catching" my gentle lobs with his belly. Basketball became a passion and he spent countless afternoons by himself, throwing the ball through the hoop. He never gave up.

James became a master of the three-point shot by the time he was a freshman in high school, but that was not enough to get him on the team. The cross-country team took all comers, however, and running was soon James' new obsession. With that distinctive run of his – one leg always a little behind – he moved up the team ranks through sheer determination. James set his sights on making the top team, on becoming one of seven runners who would compete in the state championship, his junior year in high school. I worried about the effect that disappointment might have on my son and stupidly let him know that – one of those parenting mistakes that ended with his giving me the silent treatment for two weeks while he ran harder than ever. James won his spot and by senior year, he was the top-ranked runner in his high school.

Persistence

I attended all of James' meets, until that horrible October. At work, we
had new management that did not care for lean. Actually, they were under
the impression that I was ruining the company. "Prove that this lean stuff
works," they said, "or the program is finished in six months." Meanwhile, on
a weekend visit to North Carolina to see my daughter in October, I walked
across a muddy field and got an infection in my foot that hit my body so hard,
I collapsed in the airport the following day. At the time, nobody knew that the
muddy field was to blame. There was no sign of injury. For weeks, the doctors poked and prodded, trying to understand what was wrong with me – the
fevers, spiking blood pressure, extreme lethargy – while a staph infection ate
away at the cartilage in my foot and leg.

One day, after weeks away from the office, I pulled myself together, borrowed
a wheelchair and went to work, nervous about the lean-opposition forces. It
was worse than I thought. In my absence, continuous improvement work was
being undermined throughout the organization and nobody thought it would
last two months. The following day, I was back in the hospital.

Weakened by infection, out of hope for the future, I sat there slumped in the
hospital bed waiting for an operation that I did not believe would actually fix
me. When James came to visit, I told him it felt like something essential was
slipping away from me or being stolen. I was not even sure I would have a job
to return to, if I ever got better. All of my hard work seemed be circling the
drain.

James sat beside me on the hospital bed, slipped an arm around my shoulders
and said, "Just keep trying, Dad. That's what you always told me. You've got to
keep at it, no matter what anyone says."

This bit of advice was from my son who had just come from helping his
cross-country team win the Florida state championship.

According to the apocryphal wisdom of Albert Einstein, the definition of
insanity is doing the same thing over and over and expecting different results.
The definition of persistence, meanwhile, is to keep coming at problems with

energy and intelligence, working toward a better outcome. If there is a fine line between persistence and insanity, I learned the right side to be on from watching my son.

When staying persistent starts to seem like the definition of insanity, however, it would be helpful to remember the trials of Abraham Lincoln. Born into poverty, he worked from a young age to help support the family. His mother died young, as did his first fiancee. Twice, he started businesses that failed. In 1848, two years after finally winning a seat in the U.S. Congress, he was out of a job again, having pledged to serve just one term. He followed that with two failed races for the U.S. Senate. In all, he lost eight elections at the state or national level.

Or think about Shahid Khan, arriving in Lincoln's adopted home state of Illinois in 1967 during the worst snowstorm in state history. He was a 16-year-old kid from Pakistan, in the U.S. to get an education, and he had never seen snow. He had $500 and a small suitcase. Looking for a $2 room at the YMCA, walking through the dark snowy streets, his flimsy shoes melted right off his feet. The next day, he counted himself lucky to get a job washing dishes in a Greek restaurant for $1.20 an hour. Better yet, think of Khan a dozen years later. Having graduated from the University of Illinois at Champagne-Urbana - where he discovered football, fraternities and a talent for design engineering - with a degree in engineering, he left an established automotive supplier called Flex-N-Gate to start his own company. Khan's innovation was the seamless bumper that he designed. He called his new company Bumper Works. In 1978, Khan had four employees, a pending lawsuit from Flex-N-Gate – filed as an impediment, since he was now competing against his former employer – and one big customer: General Motors Corp.

Khan's bumper was fantastic. It was a game-changing idea, GM executives assured him. In fact, GM intended to apply the seamless bumper idea to every car line. Of course, Khan's Bumper Works was not big enough to handle such a challenge, so he was politely shown the door.

In retelling this story, Khan still pauses here as if the wind has just been knocked out of him – but only for a moment. At the time, GM was also partnering with Isuzu Motors Ltd. in the sales and manufacturing of Isuzu trucks, which Khan thought would be a good fit for his bumpers. Would GM at least offer him a name, a contact at Isuzu?

Khan turned that one point of contact into a relationship, and then into more relationships. He became a frequent flyer to Japan and began supplying bumpers to a small number of Toyota pickups in 1984. By then, Khan had purchased his first employer, Flex-N-Gate, and folded in the Bumper Works operation.

Khan's company was ambitious. By 1987, Flex-N-Gate was the sole supplier of bumpers for Toyota pickup trucks and in 1989, it became the bumper source for all Toyotas made in the U.S. But Flex-N-Gate was still running batch operations. Khan had plenty of exposure to the Toyota Production System, he told Jones and Womack in *Lean Thinking*, but did not really understand it: "The light didn't come on; I really couldn't figure out how they could stay in business using the strange practices I saw."[50]

In 1989, Toyota began sending *sensei* – teachers – from its Operations Management Consulting Division to teach Khan and Flex-N-Gate how to create flow, reduce setup time and respond to customer pull. Khan spent the next three years remaking his company – and manufacturing, as he knew it – until he had one of the first truly lean companies in North America.

"We were vertically integrated. We had chrome polishing, painting, everything under one roof," Khan recalled with pride. "It was phenomenally difficult. But it worked. Until about 2000, we were masters of the universe.

"Then the market changed to plastic and everything we knew about bumpers was meaningless."

Khan and Flex-N-Gate understood steel – sourcing it, stamping it, painting it or covering it with chrome. Plastic was a different universe. So, that could have

---

50. Womack and Jones, *Lean Thinking*. 69

been the moment when he walked away, Khan said. The market was changed. He was not sure the world needed another plastic bumper manufacturer in 2000. What could Flex-N-Gate offer to customers?

Persistence, it turned out, was one thing Khan had in ample supply – and a company that still knew how to be flexible. He found a Japanese company in Canada that was making plastic bumpers but not doing very well. Khan was pretty sure he could turn it around, while he and his Flex-N-Gate team learned everything they could about plastics manufacturing.

"What we needed to do, more than anything, was to go back to what we had learned about human nature (during the original conversion to continuous improvement). And we found that certain fundamentals had been ingrained: we had to find the right people and empower them. We had to make sure we found the line between delegating tasks and abdicating responsibility," Khan said. "Lean is a test of leaders. As that water level goes down and rocks are exposed, leaders are tested."

Persistence means showing up every day, willing to tackle the problems afresh – even when your entire company seems outmoded. It means knowing that roadblocks, failures and sudden shifts in the market are all learning opportunities; and failure is just an indicator, not a terminal point.

"The most powerful thing I have found in American culture is the willingness to learn from failure," Khan said. "Look at the portfolio of any good venture capitalist in Silicon Valley. You will find more failure than success. They know that failure is not necessarily a bad thing.

"In other cultures, failure has been regarded as catastrophe, an embarrassment worthy of suicide."

If we let embarrassment or regret overwhelm us following a failure, Khan said, we lose the opportunity to learn and then move on. Failure, he likes to say, is like a merit badge for the next opportunity.

Persistence

Had Khan been completely undone by early failures, such as losing his one big customer or not responding quickly enough to major materials changes in the industry, Flex-N-Gate would not employ the 14,000 people it does in 48 manufacturing plants in the U.S. and elsewhere in the world. It would not be bringing in $3 billion in annual revenue. And Khan probably would not have realized his dream of owning a National Football League team – another feat of persistence.

Having fallen for the game while studying engineering at the University of Illinois at Champagne-Urbana, he first started talking to the NFL about team ownership in 2007. By 2010 he was ready to make a move and entered a deal to buy 40 percent of the St. Louis Rams. At the last minute, however, the majority owner exercised his right to buy the team outright. Disappointed, Khan kept looking to the next opportunity. About 18 months later, he was in serious talks with Wayne Weaver, owner of the Jacksonville Jaguars (my home team). The two men met in a bar, drew up their agreement on a napkin, and in November 2011, Khan made headlines across the country as the first person of minority status to own an NFL team.

"I think it was F. Scott Fitzgerald who said that there are no second acts in American lives," Khan said with a chuckle, "but there are. There certainly are."

Comparing timelines with Khan, I realized that – however fleetingly – quitting crossed our minds around the same time. 2000 was a difficult year. After those long weeks of a mysterious, life threatening illness, surgeries and physical therapy, I went back to work with the distinct sense that I was not wanted in some quarters. Why not walk away?

For me, persistence came from a sense of responsibility to the people who worked with me in Operations. These were people who put in their extra time and talents to make a difficult transition to lean thinking. For a couple of years they had been pushing their own limits, learning new tools and theories, and believing that their ideas were critical to our success. I did not want that taken away. My own job might be in jeopardy, but I felt answerable for their security.

Limping around the factory floor after my long absence, the question for me became how to secure the future of the Jacksonville plant? I did the only thing that made sense: Push harder.

Gathering together my team of direct reports, I described the situation as a burning platform. If we did not show real results soon, our work would consist of dismantling the improvements that we knew were the right direction and going back to the feverish pace of chaos. We needed show-stopping results within the next few months and we needed to prove those results affected the bottom line.

We pulled together the maps of our value streams – all showing the current state – and created idealized future states. Then we created implementation plans to bring us to those future states in months instead of *someday*. We listed the necessary improvement events and assigned leadership within the group. We talked about ways to resolve, on the spot, the inevitable issues that are created by improvement events, instead of waiting for follow-up work. Our main thrust would be taking away any problems that got in the way of improvements, we decided.

It was an aggressive plan, but we were determined to prove that we were right. Within weeks, we started seeing real results and then it was like eating popcorn: We just wanted more. By the summer of 2001, even the company's top brass was noticing that Operations was running very well, despite the demands of new products being introduced and larger orders coming in. The improvements would not last, they said. It was a fluke, a trick of the numbers.

Then, I found a secret weapon: Debra Rosamilia, manager of Cost Accounting. Every lean effort needs someone like Debra. An objective reporter willing to dig deep into the numbers, to look at what might have been in addition to what *is*, Debra made it absolutely clear to everyone that we were not playing games with our numbers. She put together graphs that showed current production costs compared to what costs would have been using the same old processes. She documented better quality and reduced lead times.

Persistence

Late that year, I saw another good way to put Debra's hard work to good use. We entered the competition to be recognized as one of *IndustryWeek* magazine's best plants and used her reports to help document Jacksonville's improvements in quality, cost, yield[51], customer service and scrap reduction over a three-year period. In 2002, we won the magazine's honor.

The following year, after more improvements, reports and site visits, Medtronic's Jacksonville plant won The Shingo Prize for operational excellence. Finally, it seemed as though we had achieved a measure of safety for the future of the Jacksonville plant, and for the entire lean effort.

During the most trying times in those years, when I felt like my energy and resolve was flagging, I could always turn to our 16th president for inspiration. Other presidents have been smart and eloquent. Others have led the nation during times of critical peril. But nobody else has shown as much white-knuckle persistence as Lincoln.

So much has been written about Abraham Lincoln's accomplishments during his presidency that it's easy to forget how many times he tried and failed at gaining public office earlier in his career. Lincoln ran and lost more political campaigns than he ever won. When voters spurned him, he would fall into a deep depression[52], but fought harder to win the next election.

Lincoln lost his first bid for the Illinois Legislature in 1832. At 23, he was still green for the job, and in the middle of the campaign he left to fight Native Americans in the Black Hawk War. Lincoln lost the election, finishing eighth out of 15 candidates overall. But he was encouraged by the support of his fellow residents in Salem, where he received more than 92 percent of the 300 votes cast.[53] In his second campaign for the state legislature two years later, Lincoln won.

After he left the Illinois Legislature in 1842, he was passed over by fellow

---

51. Yield refers to the number or percentage of good parts produced by a process.
52. George S. McGovern and Arthur M. Schlesinger, *Abraham Lincoln: The American Presidents Series* (Times Books, 2008) 4
53. Robert J. Johnson, Jr., *Trial by Fire: Abraham Lincoln and the Law* (ProQuest, 2007) 24

members of the Whig party for nominations he sought both for the state legis-
lature and the governorship of Illinois. He ran for Congress and lost in 1843,
then tried again in 1846 and won. He only served the one term, however, as he
had sworn not to run for re-election. Before his congressional term ended in
March 1849, Lincoln lobbied to become commissioner of the General Land
Office, a position responsible for distributing all public lands in the state of
Illinois. He lost that bid, but was offered a position as governor of the Oregon
Territory. He turned that down and returned to his law office in Springfield.

During this time, Lincoln's ambitions for public office never faded. Lincoln
campaigned fiercely against the expansion of slavery in the West, and he
lobbied behind the scenes to return to Washington, D.C., as a senator. He
came out of political retirement in 1854 and 1858, when he ran for the Senate
before losing both campaigns.

While in Congress, Lincoln had supported the Wilmot Proviso, which kept
slavery out of the territories the United States had acquired from Mexico. Lincoln was perturbed about his senate rival Stephen Douglas' refusal to acknowledge the "monstrous injustice of slavery," especially Douglas' support of the
Kansas-Nebraska Act of 1854,[54] which allowed slavery to spread in what had
been free states. After a series of now-famous debates, Lincoln lost the U.S.
Senate nomination in 1858. He was dejected after his defeat. On his way back
to his office, Lincoln slipped on a footpath and almost landed in the mud.

"The path was worn hog-back and was slippery," he recalled later. "My foot
slipped from under me, knocking the other out of the way, but I recovered
myself and lit square and I said to myself, 'It's a slip and not a fall.'"[55]

It was as if he was describing both his political career and the fierce internal
battles he faced. In the midst of his failure, he grappled with the fear that his
colleagues or voters would abandon him. Still, the next year he ran for the
presidency as a member of the newly formed Republican Party and won.

---

54. Goodwin, *Team of Rivals.*160-166 and Michael Burlingame, *The Inner World of Abraham Lincoln* (University of Illinois Press, 1997) 28
55. Michael Burlingame, *Lincoln and the Civil War* (Southern Illinois University Press, 2011) 118

Persistence

The year 1864 tested Lincoln's persistence once more. Lincoln was up for re-election, and he was worried that he would lose the vote because of growing anti-war sentiment. In July 1864, in an interview with a correspondent from the Boston Journal, the writer remarked to Lincoln that he was working too hard. Lincoln said he was worried he would lose the vote.

"Things look badly, and I can't avoid anxiety. Personally, I care nothing about a re-election, but if our divisions defeat us, I fear for the country," he told the correspondent.[56]

Things did indeed look gloomy for Lincoln. Members of Lincoln's party and even his cabinet did not support his effort to win a second term. Lincoln's former general, George B. McClellan, whom the president had fired in 1862, was running against him as a candidate for the Democrats. Even U.S. Treasury Secretary Salmon P. Chase wanted the presidency for himself. Senator Benjamin Wade criticized Lincoln's reconstruction plan, and *New York Tribune* Editor Horace Greeley, a former friend of Lincoln, believed Lincoln could not win the war, saying: "We must have another ticket to save us from utter overthrow."[57]

A number of Republicans splintered off and formed their own party, nominating military officer John C. Fremont for president. But Republicans loyal to Lincoln rebranded themselves as the National Union Party and nominated Lincoln as their candidate. To garner support among his critics, Lincoln signed a pledge on August 23, 1864, to defeat the Confederacy, even if he was defeated, and to fight until the president-elect got into office.

To further broaden his support, Lincoln replaced Vice President Hannibal Hamlin with Andrew Johnson, a pro-Union Southerner from Tennessee and a leading member of the Democrats, as his running mate.

---

56. Henry Jarvis Raymond and Francis Bicknell Carpenter, *Lincoln, His Life And Time: Being the Life And Public Services Of Abraham Lincoln, Sixteenth President Of The United States* (Nabu Press, 2011) 727
57. Richard Hofstadter, *Great Issues in American History Vol. II: From the Revolution to the Civil War, 1765-1865* (Vintage Books, 1958)

In the midst of campaigning, Lincoln still had a war to run and it was still going badly. When a number of governors wanted Ulysses S. Grant to send troops to suppress draft uprisings in the North instead of pursuing a fight to destroy a railroad that supplied the Confederacy, Grant refused. Lincoln refused to countermand him.

On August 17, 1864, Lincoln wired his general: "I have seen your dispatch expressing your unwillingness to break your hold where you are. Neither am I willing. Hold on with a bulldog grip, and chew and choke as much as possible."[58]

After he read the note, Grant reportedly chuckled and said, "The President has more nerve than any of his advisors."[59] A week later, Grant won the Battle of the Globe Tavern, a fight that effectively cut off supply lines to the city of Petersburg, Virginia, and beyond that, the Confederacy's only port.

It is important to remember that, in the heat of a moment, a leader's persistence can look stubborn and autocratic. What Lincoln, Shad Khan and James Bussell all had in common, I think, was an essential sensitivity to other human beings that made persistence a positive force. Persistence, after all, is always tempered with respect, purposefulness, holistic thinking and all the traits of a true lean leader.

Five Questions on Persistence

1. Can you describe a person in your organization who is a great role model for persistence?
2. How can persistence be detrimental?
3. What are some of the reasons why people give up and do not persist?
4. What situation in your career required you to demonstrate the greatest amount of persistence?
5. How do you encourage people who report to you to be persistent?

---

58. Abraham Lincoln, edited by H. Jack Lang, *The Wit and Wisdom of Abraham Lincoln as Reflected in His Briefer Letters and Speeches* (Stackpole Books, 2005) 234
59. Phillips. *Lincoln on Leadership*.135

HOLISTIC THINKER

Whenever we go about solving a complex problem, we first make a choice whether consciously or not: how to think about the problem. Out of habit or training, most of us follow one of two paths. We either think in reductionist mode, which is isolating the main problem from external forces and drilling down into the most fundamental issues; or we are more comfortable thinking holistically, in which we consider the problem in context, along with the conflicting or favorable forces throughout the system.

While each style of thinking is appropriate in different situations, the job of a lean leader is always to keep the entire system in mind and therefore, to think holistically. When teams are focused on improving final assembly, for instance, the leader must consider how that will effect distribution. When acquisitions are at hand, the lean leader considers existing and new cultures as well as financial statements.

To think holistically is, quite simply, to think broadly about the implications of action – or inaction – on the entire, complex, interconnected organization.

Holistic thinking is what we do as parents. Think about a teenage son or daughter standing there with one hand out, waiting for car keys. In that moment, whether conscious of it or not, a hundred considerations fly through a parent's mind because there are many possible benefits and risks. We might weigh issues as diverse as homework, health, independence, self-esteem and destination. And who are Bobby or Susie's new friends, really? If we only considered the state of that child's homework, down to the last math problem and civics essay, we would be skipping valuable information about that child's state of mind. If the teen's self-esteem was all we cared about, there is a good chance that boy or girl would not be very well balanced or prepared for the larger world.

Holistic thinking is an especially important habit for the lean leader because an organization committed to continuous improvement is constantly changing – much like that teenager – and is therefore always in danger of being thrown out of balance.

This particular trait is an internal one, part of the on-going conversations that take place in our heads. So, what does a holistic thinker look like? Will there be signs or indicating characteristics?

Paul O'Neill is not a lean promoter. He does not espouse Six Sigma. A long-time advocate of continuous improvement in general, O'Neill will not claim that any of the Deming-inspired improvement methods are the one true path either, despite the fact that he is a member of the advisory board at Columbia Business School's W. Edwards Deming Center for Quality, Productivity, and Competitiveness and is co-chair of the Deming Cup Initiative. Still, he is one of my favorite examples of a surprisingly holistic thinker.

Former secretary of the U.S. Treasury and CEO of Alcoa Inc. during its most dynamic period of growth, O'Neill is a surprise holistic thinker because, on the face of it, one might think he was single-minded. This is the man who took over the helm of the venerable but troubled Alcoa in 1987 and told a room full of Wall Street investors that his top concern was worker safety.

O'Neill had been recruited to Alcoa after several years in which the world's largest bauxite miner and aluminum producer had suffered from management missteps. Investors were anxious to be reassured. O'Neill's announcement that worker safety would be the company's focus was met with silence. He continued by pointing out the emergency exits in the room and explaining the safest way to exit, if necessary.

Finally, a couple of investors asked O'Neill the usual questions about inventories and capital ratios. O'Neill said, "I'm not certain you heard me. If you want to know how Alcoa is doing, you need to look at our workplace safety record. If we bring our injury rates down … it will be because the individuals at this company have agreed to become part of something important. They've devoted themselves to creating a habit of excellence. Safety will be an indicator that we're making progress in changing our habits across the entire institution. That's how we should be judged."[60]

In that statement is the clear marking of a holistic thinker. O'Neill was talking about safety within the context of changing the habits of the entire institution. Worker safety would be the lever to create that change.

It is important to note that Alcoa's safety record was not bad. Employees in 1987 suffered 1.87 lost workdays per 100 people per year. The national average was about five workdays lost per 100 people per year. O'Neill was not interested in how well Alcoa was doing comparatively, however.

O'Neill has always been a list writer. From the days of his first job as a construction engineer in Alaska, to working in the Veterans Administration and leading the U.S. Office of Management and Budget as deputy director, he wrote lists detailing the good and bad aspects of organizations. Finally, the lists crystalized into a to-do list for the day that he was in charge. By the mid-1980s, there were just two items:

1. All activities should be aligned around meritorious goals, such as habitual excellence.
2. There should be no internal friction or petty competition. No energy spent on interpersonal drama.

At Alcoa, with its 61,000 employees located in 31 countries around the world, O'Neill set about creating the world he wanted. "Every annual report says the same thing: 'People are our most valuable resource.' I wanted to lead an organization where that was actually true and we had the facts to prove it," O'Neill said.

---

60. Charles Duhigg, *The Power of Habit: Why We Do What We Do in Life and Business* (Random House, 2012) 99

Holistic Thinker

Because employees worked with molten metals, materials that arrived by the ton, and machines that could tear a person in two, accidents were considered a hazard of the job when he took the Alcoa helm. O'Neill saw that acceptance as disrespectful to the workers. To keep people safe, everyone needed to challenge every assumption about the way work was done. And not just in the smelters. Office workers lose more time to injury – bad backs, repetitive stress disorders – than many stevedores and steel workers.

So, he set a new goal for Alcoa: zero accidents. A lot of people thought that was crazy, O'Neill remembered. "I asked them, what would be an achievable goal? What about fifty percent improvement in worker safety? OK, who here will volunteer to be the person injured?"

Zero accidents was a perfectly reasonable goal because zero was the theoretical limit, O'Neill points out. And this was the idea that provided the framework for all of the improvement work at Alcoa: find the theoretical limit – the point at which one is limited by physics or God or the unknown – and push to achieve that goal.

Alcoa teams employed continuous improvement, *kanban* systems,[61] team problem solving and many other tools familiar to the lean leader in this work. But O'Neill avoided adopting any improvement system outright for fear that the jargon would exclude people. And O'Neill wanted every heart and mind on board. So, he kept pushing worker safety and that theoretical limit of zero accidents to the forefront of every discussion.

Once, at the giant smelter in Alcoa, Tennessee, O'Neill told a group of supervisors that safety was so important, it would no longer be a line item in the budget. Whatever needed to be spent to keep people safe would be spent and he expected immediate reports of all accidents. Then, O'Neill told the frontline workers that he wanted to be told immediately if there were unsafe conditions being tolerated and gave out his home phone number. A few weeks later, he got a call at home from a nervous employee in Tennessee. A conveyor

---

61. A Japanese word meaning "billboard," kanban is a visual resupply signal. Kanban cards act as scheduling indicators, telling associates what to produce, how much and when in order to resupply the system at the rate of customer demand.

belt was broken in the plant, he said, and workers were expected to lift and shove the too-heavy material across the break. Someone was sure to get hurt, the employee said. O'Neill called the plant manager immediately, told him to go stop the line and fix the conveyor and call back as soon as it was done.

"What I was driving for was an organization in which everyone can say yes to three statements, every day," O'Neill said.

1. I am treated with dignity and respect by everyone without regard to pay level or title or race, ethnicity, gender or any other qualifying condition.
2. I am given the things I need – tools, training, encouragement – to make a contribution to this organization in a way that gives meaning to my life.
3. I am recognized for what I do by someone I care about.

"Worker safety is tangible. It is easier to understand than this list," O'Neill said. "Frankly, I thought that if I brought up these more philosophical intangibles, the ideas behind these statements would be too easily dismissed."
The lean thinker knows that if one strives for perfection – for the list of intangibles, for zero accidents, for perfect quality – we cannot help but hit excellence along the way.

When O'Neill left Alcoa in 2000, the number of lost days due to accident had fallen from 1.87 per 100 workers to 0.2. More than that, he left an organization that was profoundly changed. With that focus on theoretical limits and continuous improvement, the finance department was now closing the books each month in 2.5 days instead of 11. In 1986, Alcoa recorded $264 million in net income on sales of $4.6 billion; it had 35,700 employees. When O'Neill left in 2000, Alcoa had record profits of $1.5 billion on sales of $22.9 billion and a payroll of 140,000, *BusinessWeek* magazine reported.[62] And to this day, safety is the first word spoken – and the first tab on the official company website – at Alcoa where lost days due to accident has continued to fall. As of April 2012, it was 0.106.

---

62. Michael Arndt, *Business Week*, February 5, 2001

Holistic Thinker

Paul O'Neill's turn around of Alcoa was a remarkable achievement. But we should also keep in mind that it happened over a dozen years, not overnight. The holistic thinker is a patient leader. Businesses are complex organisms. When we bring change, we must respect the time it takes for people to trust, and then to start moving together toward a new goal.

The biggest impediment to holistic thinking is the high walls we imagine between functional areas. CEOs are too often accustomed to thinking of their companies as a set of fiefdoms, an archipelago of functions. The executives who lead those functional areas see themselves as Sales or Research & Development or Production. It is easy for naturally competitive people to forget that a company has just one purpose, and that unity is more important than standing out.

This habit of thinking about a system as a collection of parts – a habit that is both reductive and competitive – is so ingrained that some leaders cannot make the switch to holistic thinking. The leaders that cannot change will listen to a CEO's introduction to lean thinking or continuous improvement as the company's destiny and see another initiative with a beginning and an end. And then those leaders return to their silos, looking for ways to improve that small patch of real estate.

At Medtronic, I spent seven years actively promoting policy deployment before getting everyone on board. It was during these years that I finally began to appreciate how deeply rooted are the silos in which we work.

I had attended a workshop through the Lean Enterprise Institute called "Seeing the Whole," based on the book by Dan Jones and Jim Womack,[63] and so I thought I knew what I did not know. But I was still so deeply rooted in my own manufacturing silo that I did not know how it sounded – creating company-wide agreement on a few key initiatives every year through policy deployment – to other leaders.

---

63. Daniel T. Jones and James P. Womack, *Seeing the Whole: Mapping the Extended Value Stream* (Lean Enterprise Institute, 2002)

So, I spent years infiltrating other functional areas where I could. I traveled with salespeople, trying to understand how they saw the manufacturing silo, how we helped and hindered their work. I dropped by Research & Development often, making sure they had help from manufacturing engineers as they brought new products closer to production phase and trying to understand how we could work together more seamlessly. I made new friends in customer service and accounting. People told me I seemed to be everywhere at once. There were times when I overstepped my bounds and faced forceful pushback.

In the end, it was seven years before the leaders of all Medtronic functional areas agreed to make strategic decisions together. Never underestimate the difficulty of getting people to see outside their silo walls. It must be done, however, because internal relationships and trust are as integral to the smooth operations of a business as anything else. The holistic thinker knows that keeping vital connections between business functions strong is an important aspect of the job.

This idea that the connections between the parts is critical to the survival of the whole is one that I am quite sure Abraham Lincoln understood as he stood in front of a map of these United States – a very different map than the one we know today. There was the Mason-Dixon Line and the bloody conflict taking place for the soul of the U.S. There were the big cities of the Northeast, sometimes overflowing with new immigrants and ethnic tensions. And there was the wide West: lightly populated, waiting to be stamped with the culture and beliefs of new settlers. Would western states be more connected to the Union or the Confederacy?

The Republican Party was founded in 1854 on a platform, in part, to limit the westward expansion of slavery into the frontier states. The son of frontier farmers, Lincoln also supported legislation that would help those settlers make a living.

So, in May and July of 1862, Lincoln signed four critical pieces of legislation that made it clear he was still seeing the whole United States: the Pacific Railroad Act, the Homestead Act, the Morrill Act, and finally, an act creating the Department of Agriculture. Together, this legislation made it possible for America's westward expansion to strengthen new support for the Union and for Lincoln's administration. Any one of these acts alone might have been historic, but together they served as the building blocks for a new agricultural frontier and to educate the workforce behind it.

On May 20, 1862, Lincoln signed the Homestead Act, which promised to grant 160 acres of free land in the West to anyone who could live on it and improve it for five years – including women, free African-Americans and former slaves.

President James Buchanan vetoed earlier versions of the Homestead Act, the final one in 1860 only a few months before Lincoln won the presidency.[64] Many people in the East – subsistence farmers and recent immigrants seeking new opportunities in the West -- had supported the fledgling Republican Party on the promise that the new party would free up land for settlement.[65] When Lincoln won in 1860, he seized the opportunity to create new territories in the West free of slavery, where he could also appointment friendly governors and other officials to bolster the party's anti-slavery stance and economic goals.

The act still is lauded today for fueling the growth of an agrarian middle class,[66] and condemned by others for forcing Native American tribes off lands granted in earlier treaties and pushing many tribes into poverty and war and some, into extermination. But one thing is clear, without the promise of government subsidies, free land and a network of new settlements, the railroads would not have been built in the West.

Unlike towns in the East, which were connected and crisscrossed by railroads, the west was largely wide open and unpopulated. Railroads, Lincoln believed, would keep that wild land connected to the rest of the U.S. In fact, he was dubbed the "Railroad President" during his campaign. So, about six weeks

---

64. Ralph McGinnis and Calvin N. Smith, *Abraham Lincoln and the Western Territories* (Nelson Hall Inc., 1994) 30
65. Goodwin, *Team of Rivals*. 267
66. Center for American Progress. The Top 10 Middle Class Acts of Congress. http://www.americanprogress.org/issues/2012/01/middle_class_acts.html

after signing the Homestead Act, Lincoln signed the Pacific Railroad Act "to aid in the construction of a railroad and telegraph line from the Missouri River to the Pacific Ocean" through land grants and government bonds. Westward expansion became the American destiny.

One day after signing the Pacific Railroad Act, Lincoln took up his pen again, this time for the Morrill Act, making land grants to states that established a network of agricultural colleges. Those college land grants helped create educated farming communities and launched what would become some of the largest universities in the country, including the Universities of California, Minnesota, Missouri and Wisconsin. In the east, they include Auburn University in Alabama and Rutgers University in New Jersey. Some of these Agricultural and Mechanical Colleges (called A&Ms in many states) still exist today in states such as Iowa, Oklahoma, Texas and Florida.

Many of these colleges partnered with the U.S. Department of Agriculture,[67] established by Lincoln on May 15, 1862, to create cooperative extension offices that encouraged experimentation and research at land-grant universities. Intended as a resource to help farmers large and small find improved methods for growing healthy crops, Lincoln called the USDA "the people's department." While the USDA has not had a spotless record in that regard – and was forced to settle lawsuits with African American farmers that showed long-standing patterns of discrimination – it has been credited with supporting the growth of a successful agrarian society, especially during hard times such as the Great Depression.

Lincoln understood the need to link homesteading, farm support, transportation and communication efforts in the drive to settle the West. Those interconnected pieces of legislation shaped half the country.

In strategy deployment, or *hoshin kanri*,[68] leaders face the same challenges Lincoln did: deciding how to act for the good of the whole, not just respond-

---

67. Goodwin, *Team of Rivals*. 461
68. This Japanese term essentially means to manage an organization's direction or focus. It is a method for deciding strategic goals and emphasizes selection of a very few key initiatives on which to spend time and resources.

ing to emergencies on the battlefront. It is the way we respond to areas that are not in crisis that can have the biggest impact.

To avoid the trap of reductive thinking, lean leaders should find a method for looking horizontally across value chains and the whole organization – from customer order to complete satisfaction – on a regular basis as they search for improvement opportunities. This will help leaders and subordinates alike to engage in holistic thinking. As part of this effort, look for ways to make these horizontal surveys into standard work, so that holistic thinking can become an ingrained pattern. Creating an organization-wide habit of holistic thinking should be the goal of every leader.

Five Questions on Holistic Thinking

1. What are some of the challenges you must overcome to be a more holistic thinker?
2. What barriers to holistic thinking can you break down for your team?
3. Think about the best role model you have for holistic thinking. How would you describe his or her approach?
4. How do you know when you have fallen away from holistic thinking? What are the signs?
5. How can you help others hone their holistic thinking skills?

PROBLEM SOLVER

It was March 5, 1861, the day after his triumphant inauguration. Abraham Lincoln sat down and read the report of Major Robert Anderson, commander of Fort Sumter in South Carolina, and truly began his presidency. Without fresh supplies, Anderson wrote, he would soon be forced to abandon the fort – one of the last federal properties still flying the U.S. flag in the newly formed Confederate States of America.

Sitting the middle of Charleston's harbor, within sight of where the first secessionist vote was proudly held, Fort Sumter and its U.S. flag were a constant rebuke to Confederates. How could they claim sovereignty with the stars and stripes flying in their midst? Hope for legitimacy in the eyes of European allies demanded the flag's removal. North and South glared at each other over Fort Sumter's brick walls, each asserting their rights but reluctant to take on the moral hazard of firing the first shot, of being forever perceived as the aggressor. After all, eight slave-holding states had not yet voted on secession. Their loyalty hung in the balance.

Confederate troops had turned away a supply ship bound for Fort Sumter two months earlier. The situation was now dire and Maj. Anderson reported that his supplies would not last longer than six weeks.

Lincoln turned to his cabinet with the question: Should they create conflict by attempting to resupply the fort, or peacefully withdraw, possibly giving legitimacy to the rebels? Army General Winfield Scott argued that Fort Sumter must be abandoned, as there was not enough time to prepare for the full-scale invasion needed to protect it. Postmaster General Montgomery Blair, a staunch abolitionist and Lincoln ally, argued forcefully that the Union must give no ground. Secretary of State William H. Seward urged appeasement, arguing that withdrawal from Fort Sumter might keep the remaining slave states in the Union. As for Lincoln, he received Anderson's report one day after proclaiming in his inaugural address that secession was "the essence of anarchy" and that it was his duty to "hold, occupy, and possess the property belonging to the government." Appeasing the South would surely lose him the trust of the North.

With so much riding on one decision, Lincoln decided to do something that today's lean leader would recognize as *going to gemba*. Due to the risk of assassination, he could not go to South Carolina himself, but he sent trusted emissaries to gather information both from Fort Sumter (which he repeatedly referred to as Sumpter) and the city of Charleston. Little is known of what those emissaries reported, but we do know that in early April, as Maj. Anderson was still holding Fort Sumter and watching as Confederate forces built and reinforced artillery batteries around the harbor, Lincoln authorized a flotilla carrying relief supplies. Then he carefully informed South Carolina's Governor Francis Pickens of his decision, calling the supplies "food for hungry men." He even gave a date of the ships' expected arrival.

According to Pulitzer-prize winning historian James McPherson, "This notification put the burden and stigma of starting a war on the Confederates. In effect, Lincoln flipped a coin and told Jefferson Davis 'Heads I win, tails you lose.' ... The Confederate government did not hesitate: they ordered the guns to fire on Fort Sumter even before the supply ships arrived. This action united the North and placed the stigma of starting a war on the South. 'Remember Fort Sumter' became a Northern slogan comparable to 'Remember Pearl Harbor' for Americans in World War II."[69]

Knowing that he could no longer avoid the biggest problem – War Between the States – Lincoln salvaged what advantage he could from the remaining choices at Fort Sumter.

---

69 "5 Questions for James McPherson on Abraham Lincoln and his Legacy," Encyclopedia Britannica Blog, *Facts Matter*, February 11, 2009. Accessed at http://www.britannica.com/blogs/2009/02/an-interview-with-james-mcpherson-pulitzer-prize-winning-historian-britannica-contributor-on-abraham-lincoln-his-legacy/

One hundred and forty two years later and 240 miles south of Fort Sumter, Jacksonville Sheriff John Rutherford had problems that would have made Lincoln wince. Newly elected to lead the consolidated police and sheriff offices in Duval County, Florida, where he had worked for 28 years, Sheriff Rutherford was well acquainted with the issues he faced. At least, he thought he was.

Once called the murder capital of Florida, Jacksonville was tight on resources and the department had been lumbering along with the same antiquated command structure since 1968. Span of control was being seriously violated – meaning that other police departments might have 12 officers reporting to a supervisor, while Jacksonville typically had dozens of officers for every supervisor. The jail was so overcrowded that it was a safety hazard. There were neighborhoods that seemed impenetrable to officers, and which bore the brunt of the violence.

Determined to modernize law enforcement in Jacksonville, Sheriff Rutherford began by investigating the current situation. He initiated a study of murder patterns in the county and hired a forensic auditor to look closely at how money flowed in the department. Almost immediately, the auditor found an anomaly: not all of the money from auctions and seized-asset sales seemed to be making it to the bank. As much as a half-million dollars was missing.

"Now, in modern departments, you generally see modern accounting practices. But here, we had one guy collecting all the money and making all those deposits. One guy. So we opened his office and found a four-drawer file cabinet in there, with his own bar lock on it. Inside those drawers was $562,000 in cash," Rutherford said, still sounding astonished years later.

"I turned to the auditor and said, 'How can money just get leaked out of the system like this for years without somebody noticing? How can we make sure this doesn't happen again?' That's when I heard about lean."

The auditor's husband worked for the Jacksonville Electric Authority, a not-for-profit, city-owned utility that was also a member of the Jacksonville Lean Consortium. The Consortium is a group that I helped create, bringing together

Jacksonville companies that are undergoing lean transformations to help and support each other. The auditor thought that lean practices could help Sheriff Rutherford gain control of his processes. The sheriff took the initiative and soon, I was sitting in his office talking about how lean might be applied to law enforcement. I can honestly say that I had no idea how far he would take it.

"Before I was elected to the job, I had been thinking a lot about how to lead and something that Notre Dame football coach Lou Holtz said really stuck with me. He said that everybody on a team has three basic questions for each other and their leaders: Can I trust you? Are you committed to excellence? Do you care about me?

"I immediately saw that lean could help me create an environment where everyone could answer these questions in the affirmative. Team problem solving would help us create trust. Stretch goals prove our commitment to excellence, and empowering people to create a better workplace absolutely shows that we care," Rutherford said.

In the first few years of the lean conversion of the Jacksonville Sheriff's Office, a kaizen team did a Rapid Improvement Event[70] in a copy room – where unquestioned habit had clerks copying daily reports and bulletins that went unread in that format – and saved the department the time and cost of reproducing 3.15 million copies per year. Another team made up of Rutherford's top three officers looked at the issue of crowding in the jail where inmates were overflowing the number of beds, forcing officers to set up cots in the dayroom and creating an ongoing threat to officers and each other. The team proposed a new 660-bed facility that would *almost* meet their needs at a cost of $32 million.

Reeling from sticker shock, Rutherford gave the question to a kaizen team. Here's the idea that team came up with: add another bed to each existing secure cell. The cells were big enough to accommodate two people with bunk beds. Top bunks could be made in the metal fabricating shop in one of the

---

70. As with most lean organizations, a Rapid Improvement Event in the Sheriff's Office involves a small cross-functional team tackling a defect and making immediate improvements to the process within one week.

jail facilities for less than $100 each. Total cost to build and install 864 beds: $110,000.

Jacksonville Sheriff's Office employees have not kept track of how much money they have saved with lean events. But considering the savings from the jail alone, Rutherford estimates that from 2004 to 2011, continuous improvement activities have saved the department several tens of millions of dollars. Adding up even the earliest savings, an idea took root. Rutherford could use the money saved from business processes to help fund real crime fighting. And continuous improvement would have a role there, too.

Before taking office, Rutherford read Rudy Giuliani's book, *Leadership,* and was struck by the former mayor's description of knocking down crime rates in New York City only to have them spike in nearby Newark, New Jersey. Crime was just getting pushed over a line into someone else's territory. Rutherford could not afford to play that kind of whack-a-mole, he knew, since his area of responsibility stretched 840 square miles and even if he managed to push criminals a good distance away, chances were they would still be operating in Duval County.

In 2006, a six-year study of murders in the county helped focus the issues. A pin map of where murder victims lived showed a diffuse scattering of points all across the county. A pin map of where people died, however, showed concentration in just a few trouble spots, known for drug sales. These were the problems that needed solving.

Rutherford decided that what he needed were strong, intelligence-led police units. He needed actionable, real-time data to see where problems were occurring, and to chase crime once it moved. And his officers needed a new relationship with residents.

"That old 1960s style of policing – kicking butt and taking names – that just didn't work. There's a line between protecting people and oppressing them. If you're doing something *to* people, they're going to feel oppressed. It's only when we work with people that they feel protected. I knew we had to go in and engage the community. But I didn't want to follow the community-policing model either. These neighborhoods had real problems. Going in and flipping a few burgers with them was not going to solve it.

"What we needed," Rutherford said, "was community problem solving. We needed to know what their problems were – the derelict vehicles, trash, crime, homelessness, potholes and vacant buildings – that made neighborhoods less safe. And then we needed them to help us find the solutions. They needed to own it and we needed to facilitate change. That's the only way I could see to stop being perceived as oppressors."

Rutherford hired a new data analyst and engaged a local software company to get the information officers needed. Commanders assigned a few officers to focus on the known bad elements in the trouble spots, but the majority of officers in the area were sent out to knock on doors, targeting the good people to get them involved.

Called Operation Safe Streets, the door-knocking officers handed out pamphlets with safety tips, talked about neighborhood troubles, and recruited residents to join with police in ShAdCo. The Sheriff's Advisory Councils, or ShAdCos, were the existing neighborhood groups set up by Rutherford's predecessor, but seriously underused. In all, officers knocked on 77,000 doors. Soon, there were 3,000 people participating in 19 councils serving neighborhoods all over the city.

Those ShAdCo meetings end up functioning like continuous improvement team meetings. Residents set the agenda and run the meetings and everyone – deputies included – is expected to bring in ideas for neighborhood improvements, discuss possible solutions within budgets and abilities, and then create assignments and timelines. Each of Rutherford's assistant chiefs is responsible for three ShAdCos and is expected to help direct residents toward government or private resources, if needed, to complete projects. This has created a lot of individual improvements. But perhaps more importantly, the discipline of those monthly ShAdCo meetings helped create an expectation of cooperation that serves everyone well, even during highly charged circumstances, Rutherford said.

One Mother's Day, for instance, a 13-year-old girl named Shenice Holmes was reading a book in her bedroom when the stray bullet of an ongoing drug dispute broke her window, slammed through a pillow and killed her. Sheriff Rutherford spent that day with a grieving mother, vowing to do more than just catch a killer.

At the neighborhood ShAdCo meeting, deputies and residents talked about the apartments on Harts Road where Shenice Holmes lived. Part of a small complex of apartment houses with deep porches and peeling paint, the area was known for drug sales, rival gangs and the overgrown, wooded fields that lay between apartment houses. Unlit, filled with trash and broken glass, those woods were a haven for thieves and drug runners. Cleaning that up would be a good start, neighbors said.

After working out a plan with neighbors, the Sheriff's Office arranged to have the woods and field cleared, lighting added to the area, and some landscaping put in. Using inmate labor, they even cleaned up the deep porches attached to nearby apartments that were thick with accumulated junk. Drug sales in the area plummeted. (A 21-year-old gang member who admitted firing his gun while chasing rivals that day was later sentenced to life in prison plus 60 years for Shenice Holmes' murder.)

"I tell my assistant chiefs, the one thing that I never want to hear is that a problem was brought to ShAdCo and nothing happened," Rutherford said.

In 1971, with a population of a little more than a half-million people, Duval County had 86 murders. In 2011, with the population nearly doubled, murders dropped to 72. Meanwhile, the clearance rate has steadily gone up. In 2009, the national average for police departments solving murders – the clearance rate – was 56.7. The rate for Jacksonville Sheriffs was 78.8. In 2010, their clearance rate was 82.5. In 2011, it was 83.1.

Murder rates are going down and those that do occur are getting solved at a

higher rate, Rutherford pointed out, even though his department is contract-
ing. Last year, budget priorities meant he had to lay off 129 people – 71 of
them officers – in order to save about $17 million. Service levels, he said, have
not been affected.

"This is absolutely because of ShAdCo and community involvement and lean,"
Rutherford said. "Our tips from the community are through the roof because
they know now we will do something about it. And our resources are not tied
up in wasteful business practices."

Sheriff Rutherford and Abraham Lincoln were both faced with problems in
need of immediate solutions. What ties them together – besides being newly
elected and keenly aware of their constituents' expectations – is the methodical
way they approached problem solving. Even a casual observer would have seen
each man move through a five-step process:

- Define the problem clearly
- Investigate current situation
- List all options, including the ideal
- Plan and implement solution
- Check results

How many of us, on a semi-regular basis, skip the first step entirely, skim past
the second and leap immediately to number four? Why spend time investigating the situation and considering the options if one can make an educated
guess, right? It is human nature – especially for a person called "the boss" – to
want to be the one with the answer, the savior with the right solution.

Finding the best answer in a lean world, however, requires that we collect
information, engage others in finding solutions, and always follow up on actions taken. And because we are depending on others to find those solutions,
we must have a strong and consistent method for solving problems – one that
respects the strengths and limitations of the people using it. Problem-solving
exercises in a laboratory full of Ph.D. engineers will be far different, obvi-

ously, from those used by technicians who know only high-school level math. Therefore, the only consideration in selecting a problem-solving methodology should be: Will this help our people find root cause?

At Medtronic, we kept falling short of root cause, or going off in the wrong direction. We were using DMAIC to guide problem solving, but our efforts lacked focus. For instance, we might define a problem clearly with a problem statement and a goal. Then, a continuous improvement team would go off and measure everything they could think of around that problem, making the issue too large and diffuse to solve. So, we had a team from Toyota come in to teach us problem solving. They had a great eight-step process guaranteed to help us find root cause. Only, most people could not follow through on all of those steps. The form that the Toyota team used was a confusion of tiny print running off in different directions. We wanted problem solving for everyone, not just the specialists.

Once again, we decided to go our own way — cobbling together a series of steps that made sense to all of our people and drove us to root cause. After the problem was defined, we set a goal, clearly stated the gap between reality and desired outcome, and asked the four Ws: *who, what, when, where.* Then we performed Pareto analyses and kept focusing and refining until it could be proved in a court of law. Our fictional court of law, anyway. A lot of our people were fond of law-and-order or crime-scene television shows, and we found that building a criminal case against a defect was a very useful exercise. Popular culture has made us all very aware of what it means to prosecute and defend, so we used that to full advantage.

Chuck Carlton, a Lean Sigma project manager, was a real instigator in defining our problem-solving methodology, so I will let him explain. "We told people that they had to look at those Pareto charts and build a factual case. They had to argue each side.

"So, we had motors that were overheating, for instance. There were 100 failures in the last month and we wanted zero. That was the definition. We found that, in the three motors we used, 70 percent of the failures were in motor A.

We asked *who, what, when, where* and found that failures were split between all operators and shifts. But every failure was in a particular part of the motor with four components. We became attorneys for each component, trying to prove their guilt or innocence."

Not only did team members identify the bad component, they became so interested in what caused that component's guilt – how it turned criminal – that they traced it back to the supplier and that company's manufacturing process. Then, they proved that the real culprit was a cutting blade in the fabrication area that was not sharpened often enough.

We made a couple of simple rules around problem solving at Medtronic. If there were four possible solutions and three would solve it some of the time and one would fix it every time, use the final one. Instead of trying to fix every issue that appeared in the gap analysis, fix one issue at a time. We started referring to rules like this – big issues made simple – as "Chuck It Down" rules.

Here is my favorite Chuck It Down, courtesy of Chuck Carlton: "We're not trying to solve world hunger. We are trying to find the hungriest family and feed it. It's a start."

Besides finding a good problem-solving methodology, being a lean leader means trusting that our people, using that good process, will lead us to the right solution – even if it is not exactly the Toyota way.

In 2005, for instance, Medtronic was enjoying a growth spurt. Those of us who have been in Operations during a dynamic growth period know that "enjoying" might not be the right word. Every week there were new products to incorporate into production, ballooning orders and conflicting priorities. Operations teams at five facilities across the country were struggling to understand what projects to deselect and how to align themselves to Medtronic's goals. I knew the answer was *hoshin* planning. Even though my efforts to introduce hoshin and strategy deployment to the larger business had gotten no traction, I was determined to bring this powerful tool to Operations. I learned how to use the classic X Matrix – developed in Japanese companies such as Toyota – from Danaher Corp., which had great success with the tool. That was good enough for me. Beginning in Jacksonville, I introduced the single-sheet X Matrix to help us align our priorities top to bottom, and to de-select projects that were not crucial to company goals. My team in Jacksonville carefully worked through the process, developed both hard copy and digital version of the X Matrix, distributed them throughout our areas, and was preparing to launch this in other facilities when we noticed something disconcerting. Nobody was using our carefully prepared matrix.

Virtually unreadable for our people due to its complexity, the matrix sat in books and computer files unused while people still were overwhelmed by thousands of equally important tasks. Upon investigating, I found that this powerful tool was not dynamic or engaging for people, and so it was resented as just another management initiative. And still, the work was coming at everyone as if from a fire hose. We needed a fresh take.

After a series of off-site meetings where we stepped back, restated the problem, investigated the current situation and starting listing the options, we ditched the X Matrix and took a road trip to Mystic, Connecticut. There, in another Medtronic facility, Scott Quaratella, Mystic's director of Operations, built a giant white board out of painted sheet metal so we could stick things to it with magnets. Together, the plant directors and top managers built our own kind of hoshin planning that would make sense to us.

While the entire company was not represented in those meetings, we tried to make sure the whole organization's needs where considered. We took Medtronic's mission statement as the true north and broke out five key result areas – finance, new products, quality, customer service and human development – on which to focus our projects. When we had the mission-critical projects selected, we needed a policy deployment process to communicate, execute and track those projects.

Instead of one sheet of paper, we used a lot of color-coded index cards. Green cards indicated projects that were running on time and smoothly. Yellow cards revealed a missed deadline or a roadblock that was coming into view, requiring assistance. Red cards showed projects that were on the verge of failure. These cards mirrored a visual system in the plant, in which problems and possible fixes were noted on colored cards that indicated priority.

Every index card was stuck to the homemade whiteboard, and every card was backed up by an A3 that justified the resources put into the project and showed how it aligned with Medtronic goals. The A3s were all embedded in the electronic spreadsheet version of each facility's planning board, so we could all access each plant's Visual Leadership Center online, as well. Soon, every Medtronic facility from Connecticut to California had one of those homemade whiteboards in an identically set up room that became the information hub of the operation. We called it the Visual Leadership Center, where anyone could walk in and, at a glance, check the status of Operations' mission-critical projects.

Next, we set up strategy deployment boards for our individual value streams, such as electronic equipment, sterile disposable products and otology (ear products). Using the same visual cues from boards in the Visual Leadership Center and on the plant floors, we soon had everyone speaking the same language.

For the 10 years between 2002 and 2012, Medtronic's business quadrupled. While this would stress the operations of any business, we managed to be the department that most consistently met our objectives during those years. This was not due to our fancy colored index cards. We were able to do this because we solved problems together.

One caveat about the language used in this chapter: Taken too literally, the idea of being a problem *solver* can lead us down a path that is not very lean. The truth is, we never really solve a problem. Sheriff Rutherford knows that trouble spots move and conditions at the neighborhood level always need to be monitored. Abraham Lincoln knew that solving the issue of resupplying Fort Sumter – no matter which way he went – would only open a new can of worms and change the situation all over again.

We identify problems and put counter measures in place. But in a constantly changing environment, the circumstances surrounding a problem and the problem itself will likely be in flux. Maybe it will not change tomorrow or next week, but it will change and so the "fix" will need to be revisited.

This is why it is important to keep in mind that a problem solved is not a problem concluded. There will always be more – often times, too many – opportunities to practice those problem-solving skills.

Five Questions on Problem Solving

1. What steps did you follow in solving a recent critical problem?
2. What are some of your biggest issues in terms of problem solving?
3. How do you insure that you solve the root cause of problems and not just the symptoms?
4. What is your approach in training and coaching people in problem solving throughout your organization?
5. How do you measure the effectiveness of your problem solving method?

RESULTS DRIVEN

First gear on his 4-speed manual transmission Porsche tops out at 85 miles per hour. The tires are treadless race slicks. And when F. Barry Bays' 700-horsepower, custom-built GT1R rockets down the track at speeds up to 180 mph, he is grateful for the chin strap that keeps his head stable.

Yes, this is the same F. Barry Bays from chapter four, who so strongly influenced me at Xomed. In the years after leaving Xomed to become CEO of Wright Medical, Barry also took up Porsche Club Racing. Like most everything he does, Barry entered this new territory purposefully.

He started with a stock-class Porsche 911 and learned the basic driving skills at high-performance driver education events. For two years he raced that car, developing his driving skills, reading books on racing strategy and the technical aspects of controlling a car. Then he took a four-day intensive course at a professional driving school in Arizona and entered the amateur racing ranks of Porsche Club of America Racing Series. His good friend and racing partner back in Tennessee, Pat Williams, designed and built his first racer, a GT3R, and then his GT1R a few years later. All year long, Barry studies videotapes of races – his own, and those of better drivers – looking at how drivers set up the car to enter and exit a turn, and for braking and acceleration points. When he is not racing, he lifts weights and does cardiovascular workouts to keep in good physical condition. After all, most of the other drivers are 10 to 15 years younger than Barry and he knows reaction time can mean the difference between being a champion and wrecking his car.

So, when the car just ahead of him goes into a spin at full race speed, Barry is grateful for the countless hours of groundwork he puts into every race –

the meticulous car preparation, the tracks studied, the physical and mental toughness – that allow him to twist the wheel, punch the gas, avoid a collision and feel a burst of adrenaline that is like nothing else in the world.

"Preparing for a race is no different than preparing a business for a results-driven outcome," Barry said. "There is no difference at all."

In a lean environment, the definition of *results driven* is often quite different than in a traditional company. In most companies, results sought are stated as goals that are set by top managers who then remind everyone of the goals at every turn. Billboards are erected showing progress toward the goals. Employee assessments and profit sharing hinge on achieving the goals. *How* people arrive at the goals appear less important than hitting the mark. Traditionally, being results-driven leads to a make-the-month mentality in organizations, creating an endless cycle of demand bulges and anxiety. That is not what we mean by *results driven*.

For lean practitioners, being results driven means focusing on the process instead of the outcomes, because we all know that it is the process – not the goal – that produces results. To arrive at a successful finish, in other words, we focus on the middle distance, not the end.

I like to use the analogy of a tennis player; racquet in hand, aching to win this closely matched set. If she worries about checking the scoreboard, she will miss the play and lose the game. The smart player knows to focus her energy on the ball and the other player, to play her best game and let the score take care of itself.

This is not to say that goals and scoreboards are unnecessary for the results-driven leader. We must define our destination before we start the trip, after all. Barry Bays started his racing career with results in mind. He wanted to drive very fast, do it safely, and win races. Like a good lean thinker, he defined his goals and then turned his full attention to establishing and improving his processes.

It should surprise nobody that the process of identifying goals and improving processes used by a good results-driven leader like Barry looks a lot like DMAIC.

- Define the desired results.
- Measure the current situation by drawing out a current-state map or, depending on the situation, use another measuring tool or chart.
- Analyze the gap between desired results and future state; list all options for closing the gap.
- Create and execute an improvement plan.
- Create controls in the process to make improvements stick.

"Being results driven is all about sticking to the game plan," Barry said. "There are no shortcuts."

Focusing on process and paying meticulous attention to detail certainly paid off for Barry. In 2011, he earned the title of National Champion in his car class. Just eight years after he began racing, facing a field of much younger people, he was the top Porsche GT1R racer in the country.

If Barry took shortcuts in planning for a race, he would put his entire team at risk of more than just losing a race. In a business setting, the effect is similar. Taking shortcuts leads to errors and lack of control. Shortcuts put quality at risk and – because shortcuts are so rarely documented – it almost always costs more time later as others try to sort out what happened.

One of the hardest jobs of a lean leader is to be consistently systematic in approach, and to teach teams the same discipline. Without that discipline, I have found that chaos and headaches are the inevitable result.

Before Barry arrived at Xomed, for instance, we had one of those demand bulges that are often the hallmark of a growing company. Xomed had just entered a new market channel with a popular line of battery-powered devices that burned away flesh with electrical currents. Called a cautery, these devices are critically important in many types of surgery where doctors want to cut away diseased flesh or coagulate it to stop bleeding. Xomed's small, cordless cauteries gave surgeons great flexibility and they were immediately popular in these new distribution channels.

Demand for the devices jumped by 50 percent. My team and I did exactly what anybody – we thought – would do in the event of such a demand spike: we threw a bunch of extra help into cautery assembly and authorized plenty of overtime. *Make more*, we said. Production rose accordingly. And then, like a snake trying to swallow the moon, everything came to a sudden halt.

Having failed to think through the entire cautery production process, we were surprised by a choke point downstream. After assembly, cauteries needed to be sterilized and packaged. The sterilizing equipment required seven days to run a full cycle. This long processing time had been figured into production scheduling on all products, but had not been considered for meeting this sudden demand increase. Not only were cauteries not getting through at an acceptable rate, cauteries were dominating the sterilizer and pushing out other products that also required sterilization. Suddenly, there was chaos in several product lines, inventory was piling up at the sterilizer, and orders were getting lost between assembly and shipping.

That chaos was the result of traditional thinking. A goal was handed down – 50 percent more cauteries – and then management (me) focused just on making those numbers. Fortunately, my team and I were far enough into lean thinking that we quickly realized our mistake and refocused on the process.

In this case, the sterilizer was an obvious choke point that needed greater speed and flexibility. Our investigation revealed that actual sterilization occurred much faster than the seven-day cycle time. Sterilization actually happened in less than one day, but products were required to remain in the unit to test for growth of microbiological material. We could, however, switch to a process called parametric release – which would require a lot of testing and verification and finally, Food and Drug Administration approval – that would cut sterilizer cycle time down to a single day. In the end, it took an entire year to switch to parametric release and cut the sterilizer cycle time, but at least we were able to begin moving in that direction.

Looking back, I realized that this was one of those serendipitous failures. Yes, my team and I were shortsighted and created a temporary mess. But in the long run, we not only created a far more efficient and flexible sterilization process, we also began taking a hard look at demand bulges to see what created them and how they might be smoothed.

In every investigation we used DMAIC and A3s, having learned – once again – that shortcuts and quick answers were a hazard. The only way to arrive at desired results is to have a reliable, repeatable approach to problem solving and to follow that approach every time. So, the next time that the vice president of sales told me that orders on a product were up 50 percent and all orders had been promised by the end of the month, we knew enough to look at the entire value chain of that product before making decisions – and to initiate talks with sales on how to smooth out those demand bulges.

The power of results-driven leadership is even easier to visualize in the arena of new product development. Barry Bays has a great example. Back when he and Jim Treace were remaking Concept, Inc. – the gulf coast of Florida medical supply company that would someday become Linvatec – they heard orthopedic surgeons complaining. Actually, it is not that unusual to hear surgeons complain. But Barry and Jim really listened, particularly to complaints about cutting instruments for arthroscopic surgery that were dull, because they thought they might be able to do something about it.

This was back in 1982, in the dawn of arthroscopic knee surgery. The knee is a watery environment and getting an electrically driven cutter to work precisely and consistently – and evacuate tissue as it worked – in that setting is a challenge. One company conquered the obstacles, created a groundbreaking device, and had the market sewn up. Almost as soon as arthroscopic knee surgery became the new craze, however, surgeons started to complain about problems with the powered instrument. The reusable blades could became unexpectedly dull due to multiple uses and, sometimes, damage during resterilization. When the instrument was redelivered into the surgical procedure, the surgeon never knew if the cutter blade would be sharp enough. The instrument was not entirely reliable and too expensive – about $900 each – to replace frequently.

Jim and Barry listened to the complaints and decided to create a better cutter. Concept did not really have the manufacturing or the sales capability to enter this high-tech arena, but Jim and Barry thought they could work it out.

"Back then, we were becoming results driven but weren't entirely there," Barry said. "This project absolutely pushed us there."

First came the definition, as Jim and Barry began with a list of desired results. The instrument must be reliable and sharp 100 percent of the time, they said. It should be a single-use, sterile, cutting device integrated with a power-drive system that Concept, unfortunately, did not make. And just to keep everyone's eyes on costs, they decided that the targeted customer price for the final product should be $35 each.

Barry – an engineer who began his career as a machinist – gathered a team and began developing the disposable arthroscopic instrument, working methodically through the issues. Within a year, they were ready to launch and thought they could sell thousands of the devices every month. Within six months, orders were in the tens of thousands.

"If we were not results driven, we would not have been successful. And I'll tell you what was really important here – it was defining our goals and communicating exactly what we planned to do. If you send mixed signals, you'll get mixed results," Barry said. "This success started us on a roll that lasted for 10 years, (until Treace and Bays left Concept for new challenges at Xomed) and we never forgot the importance of driving for results."

If you send mixed signals, you will get mixed results. I cannot help but think that Abraham Lincoln would have liked that quote, and maybe even repeated it as the moral to one of his stories. As a lawyer, a lawmaker and a nascent military strategist, he always seemed to be operating with the end in mind, one eye on the results, but without shortchanging the process he took to get there. In my home library, I have shelves devoted to books on Lincoln and even a casual scan yields a surprising number of illustrations of a results-driven man, from areas throughout his life.

When preparing for trial, for instance, Lincoln made it a habit to argue each side instead of focusing only on his own. He was always checking the strength and validity of his own arguments against the opposition, which was, he knew, how he would be judged. As a lawmaker keenly interested in strengthening the frontier and keeping it free of slavery, he supported legislation as diverse as the Homestead and Morrill Acts and created the Department of Agriculture.

Yet, it is as a military strategist that Lincoln truly shows his results-driven side. Because the war began almost as soon as Lincoln stepped into office and he had no real military experience, Lincoln was forced to rely on the counsel of his generals who assured him it would be a short-lived campaign. The Confederates had no standing army. While many Southern leaders were West Point trained, there was no real military infrastructure in the South. Leaders of the Union Army were over confident and did not immediately press their advantage.

In that initial lull, Lincoln read everything he could find on military strategy and tactics, and watched in growing alarm as his generals amassed troops and provisions, trained soldiers and waited, even while the Confederate Army pulled together and moved northward. While Lincoln urged his generals – one after another – to engage the Confederate Army directly, they asked for additional resources and more time for training.

When the Civil War began, the entire U.S. Army had only 16,400 men and many of the men were untrained in battle, scattered at lonely frontier outposts in the West. General George McClellan claimed he could end the war in two weeks if he only had 50,000 new recruits.[71] As the Civil War dragged on, particularly into the dark days of 1862, desertions among the Union regiments

---

71. William Marvel. *Lincoln's Darkest Year: The War In 1862.* (Houghton Mifflin Harcourt, 2008.) 85

escalated. Some regiments lost as many as one out of four soldiers to desertion.[72] Lincoln desperately needed more soldiers, and to make the war and Union Army a point of Northern pride.

Because Lincoln was always operating with one eye on how his results would affect his true purpose – preserving the Union – he came at the issue of recruitment and financing of the war from multiple angles, employing several tactics.

Lincoln used his power to appoint generals as a political tool, for instance, selecting some of his generals simply because they represented immigrant groups he hoped to win over. If the general in charge seemed familiar to a group – Italian, Irish, Dutch or Scottish – families would be more willing to entrust their sons to the Army, Lincoln reasoned. These political generals did not always sit well with the West Point-educated military officers. One of Lincoln's notable political appointments was the promotion of Alexander Schimmelfennig – a well-known member of the Dutch community – to the post of brigadier general. Even Secretary of War Edwin Stanton protested Schimmelfennig's appointment, saying there were better qualified German Americans in Pennsylvania who could be named.

"No matter about that," Lincoln replied. "His name will make up for any difference there may be."[73]

By April 1862, the Union had amassed an army of 637,000. Unfortunately, Schimmelfennig's only memorable contribution was escaping from the Battle of Gettysburg in July 1862 by hiding his general's uniform under another person's coat and then evading capture by hiding in a shed for three days.

That year, 1862, was a dreadful time. A series of devastating military setbacks left the Union ranks thin. Lincoln issued a call for 300,000 more recruits and – in 1863 – instituted the nation's first military draft, a lottery that conscripted

72. Wilmer L. Jones, *Generals in Blue and Gray: Lincoln's Generals.* (Greenwood Publishing Group, 2004.) 27
73. James M. McPherson, "Lincoln as Commander in Chief." Smithsonian, January 2009, http://www.smithsonianmag.com/history-archaeology/Commander-in-Chief.html?c=y&page=2

able-bodied men between the ages of 24 and 45 into the Union Army.[74] Property-owning men, only sons and others were allowed to avoid conscription, however.[75] Wealthier families, north and south, could pay for substitute soldiers and keep their sons at home. Military service fell disproportionately on immigrants who had applied for U.S. citizenship. One out of four white soldiers were immigrants conscripted through the draft.[76] Widespread demonstrations and rioting marked that first military draft, beginning the United States' long, thorny history with forced conscription.

Where Lincoln most obviously showed his results-driven nature was, I think, in the way he kept pushing his generals to prosecute the war. McClellan and others saw the battles as on a chessboard, looking for territory to occupy and control. It was as if they were trying to skip to the end, making individual territories Union-held and thus stitching together the country again. But Lincoln urged them to fight the actual Confederates – to stay focused on the grim process of war.

In 1862, Lincoln was particularly vexed by the Confederates' long front that allowed the Southern army to quickly change their points of concentration by moving troops to hot spots from behind the safety of their protected front. He believed the Union could break the Confederate front and urged his generals to attack the line from eastern Kentucky to the Mississippi River. Lincoln repeatedly asked his officers to cut off enemy armies that had ventured northward by blocking their avenues of retreat. But both Generals Henry W. Halleck and Don Carlos Buell balked.

Lincoln's generals tried five times to break that line, during the Shenandoah Valley drive north in May 1862, the invasions of Maryland and of Kentucky in September 1862, the Battle of Gettysburg in 1862, and the raid on Washington in July 1864. After each failed attempt, Lincoln relieved generals of com-

---

74. William Marvel, *Lincoln's Darkest Year: The War In 1862* (Houghton Mifflin Harcourt, 2008) 84
75. The Confederate government also instituted a draft in 1862, with similar exceptions to military service.
76. Steven E. Woodworth, Kenneth J. Winkle, and James McPherson *Oxford Atlas Of The Civil War* (Oxford University Press, 2004) 204

mand.[77] Not until soldiers led by Ulysses S. Grant captured a key stronghold in Vicksburg, Mississippi in 1863 did Lincoln finally find a general who could mobilize his troops rapidly. Like Lincoln, Grant understood that attack rather than occupation was the key to winning the war.

At the end of his first term, there was still no end in sight. A dismayed Lincoln wrote, "War at the best, is terrible, and this war of ours, in its magnitude and in its duration, is one of the most terrible."[78]

While Lincoln focused most of his attention on how the Civil War would be won, he could not ignore the fact that it was going to be an expensive. With the secession of Southern states, revenue from the cotton trade stopped. The longer the Civil War was waged, the larger the national debt grew.

Lincoln asked Treasury Secretary William P. Chase to find new tax revenues to subsidize the war. The first Civil War tax increase was passed on August 5, 1861 and called for $20 million in new taxes from the states. Almost a year later, however, Chase decided the tax increase was not enough. In July 1862, Congress created new income and inheritance taxes and crafted the agency under the Treasury Department to enforce collection, the Office of Internal Revenue. That agency later became the Internal Revenue Service.

As military expenses skyrocketed, so did the unpopular income taxes. So the agency found new revenue sources, levying new taxes against public utilities, distilled spirits, tobacco, banks and insurance companies. There were new duties for carriages, yachts, billiard tables, gold and silver. The Treasury discovered it could tax certain retail products – an early version of the sin tax – and had taxpayers pay an extra penny for an 18-cent pack of playing cards.[79] In the rush to create new money, the U.S. Treasury that same year minted money for

---

77. James M. McPherson. "Lincoln as Commander in Chief." *Smithsonian*. January 2009, http://www.smithsonianmag.com/history-archaeology/Commander-in-Chief.html?c=y&page=2
78. Michael Perman and Amy Murrell Taylor, *Major Problems in the Civil War and Reconstruction: Documents and Essays* (Wadsworth Publishing, 2011) 217
79. Gary Giroux and Sharon Johns, "Financing The Civil War: The Office of Internal Revenue and the Use of Revenue Stamps." (Paper, Texas A&M University Department of Accounting, April 2000). Accessed May 16, 2012. http://web.acct.tamu.edu/giroux/financingcivil.htm

the first time and coined a new term for American currency – it was called the "greenback."

There are many who would criticize Lincoln's methods. But if we examine each of these actions – creating taxes to pay the Civil War's enormous bills, drafting citizens to fight side by side, and appointing generals from various ethnic groups – it is clear that he was always working to strengthen the common ties of a people fractured by war. This was a president who was always looking ahead to the results and tying them to his true purpose.

The modern CEO interested in changing her ways to become more results driven must first look to her organization's processes. Like Lincoln researching military strategy or Barry Bays studying a racetrack, the CEO must have confidence that the organization's approach to problem solving and analysis is sound, fact-based and scientific in approach. Only then will she be confident that her results will be reliable and foreseeable.

Foresight is one of those qualities we ascribe to great leaders – people who seem to see three steps past everyone else. This is not magic, however. Foresight is what happens when a leader knows and trusts his problem-solving process. With experience and vigilance, leaders will be able to see the results early and adjust the organization's reaction as results begin to unfurl, instead of waiting for the end.

The results-driven leader is also a holistic leader, working through the process with care and consideration for the entire organization, instead of throwing a bunch of individual levers as a shortcut to a quick outcome.

But the mark of a true leader is one who teaches others to see how those results unfold. In a robust organization, many people are capable of foresight and can join in the discussion of how to prepare for and redirect action to achieve the desired results. A weak organization features a know-all leader, barking orders and expecting everyone to follow without question.

Remember: Results are simply the outcome of working through a process. If that process is reliable and repeatable, the results will be far more stable and trustworthy.

Five Questions for the Results-Driven Leader

1. How do you balance the pressure of achieving short-term results with ensuring correct methods and processes?
2. How do you know that your process for achieving results is reliable and repeatable?
3. What do you feel are the key factors in achieving results on a consistent basis?
4. Can you describe one thing that you need to change in your approach to achieving results?
5. How do you communicate your expectations around achieving results?

COURAGEOUS

The chief of Medicine for the Appleton Medical Center stepped to the front of the room and faced his fellow doctors with a frown. Several patients in the Intensive Care Unit had suffered life-threatening blood-sugar spikes over the past few months. One person died. The doctors, it appeared, were delivering medical errors to their sickest patients.

This was not exactly news to the internists of Appleton Medical Center, but they shifted uncomfortably, waiting for John Toussaint to make his point.

The ICU patients in question were too incapacitated to eat and had to receive liquid nutrition intravenously. The concentrated solution of glucose and vitamins was caustic and varied wildly from one patient to the next. Every doctor, it seemed, had a different recipe for parenteral nutrition – mostly based on the particular theories that were embraced by the school he or she attended – and some of those solutions were hurting patients. Quite a few patients, actually. Every month, between 30 and 40 patients received parenteral nutrition, or TPN, and five or six of those patients experienced trauma related to it.

With so much variation in the liquid solution, a controlled investigation was just about impossible. So, Dr. Toussaint offered doctors his solution: create a common protocol. With one recipe, so to speak, they could see how patients were affected and create controlled variations for particular patient conditions based on what they learned. Dr. Toussaint even had a proposed recipe that was based on his extensive review of patient charts and consultations with the hospital's staff nutritionist, who had expertise in the subject.

The doctors scoffed. Dr. Toussaint's protocol was dismissed as "cookbook medicine." It seemed as though the chief was trying to undermine the traditional autonomy of doctors. Case closed.

At the next month's peer review meeting in that summer of 1987, the only item on the agenda – again – was the problem with TPN. Dr. Toussaint again lost his case. But it was Dr. Toussaint's job as chief of Medicine to set the agenda for peer review meetings, and so the following month TPN was again the only agenda item. And the following month, as well. When it was finally clear that Dr. Toussaint was not giving up, the doctors voted 12-11 to use the protocol. Within six months, life-threatening surges of blood sugar levels fell from an average of more than five per month to zero.

I tell this story in the chapter on courage for two reasons. The particular courage that is required to advocate for change to a room full of strong-willed peers – most of whom do not particularly see a need for change – is a common test for lean leaders. This is the kind of daily courage required in a lean environment. However, as Dr. Toussaint readily admits, this story is a good example of how *not* to be a courageous lean leader.

"Just thinking about it now, how I went before those doctors and told them that we were delivering bad medicine so this was the solution we were putting in place; well, it's embarrassing," Dr. Toussaint said. "I would not do that today."

With experience, Dr. Toussaint learned what lean leaders know – courage is embracing change that is substantive instead of incremental; it is being unafraid of failure; it is being willing to stand up to those who are risk adverse, and it is always inclusive. Courage is not about dictating course or riding off alone into the sunset.

In a lean environment, after all, courage is respectful, honest and persistent. Courage is about holistic thinking, problem solving, and each of the other characteristics too. It is not about charging ahead and presenting solutions. In Dr. Toussaint's case, that tactic earned him the resentment of his fellow doctors and, quite likely, a delay in implementing change.

"It did require some courage to step outside of the box and tell my colleagues that, no matter how good we were comparatively, we were still causing deaths that could have been prevented," Dr. Toussaint said. "But now, I would spend a lot of time getting them engaged on helping me define what the problem really was. And then I would anoint some of them to discover the root cause and come up with counter measures to fix it. Now, we use A3s, in teams, and scientific processes to fix problems."

Dr. Toussaint became chief medical officer of ThedaCare not long after that incident. A few years later he was named CEO of the ThedaCare system of hospitals, clinics, nursing homes and other cradle-to-grave health services that is the largest employer in northeast Wisconsin. Over the course of eight years at the helm, Dr. Toussaint led one of the largest lean makeovers of a healthcare system anyone has seen and is the author of two books about the experience.[80]

In that time, he learned that it is the job of a lean leader to help others find the courage to make big changes. And sometimes, it is our job to ask others for the courage to keep going.

One of my favorite stories of leadership courage happened about three years into ThedaCare's lean journey. Dr. Toussaint and his team had been dealt some powerful setbacks and grumbling among staff members had become voluble. In fact, annual surveys showed the worst employee satisfaction scores and the worst physician satisfaction scores in the history of ThedaCare's survey. Added to that, eight orthopedic surgeons had just split off to start their own clinic and surgery across town, taking away millions of dollars in revenue.

And then it was time for every CEO's favorite moment: the Board of Trustees meeting. With all those bad results in hand, Dr. Toussaint faced the board without trying to minimize the damage or lay blame elsewhere. "What could I do? I presented the worst surveys ever; I talked about the surgeons leaving. I

---

80. John Toussaint, MD and Roger A. Gerard, PhD, *On the Mend: Revolutionizing Healthcare to Save Lives and Transform the Industry,* (Lean Enterprise Institute 2010)
John Toussaint, MD, *Potent Medicine: The Collaborative Cure for Healthcare,* (Theda Care Center for Healthcare Value 2012)

said, 'It looks like I'm destroying this place. Do you want me to keep going?'"
Dr. Toussaint recalled. "I wanted to keep going, but they needed to know that
things were likely to get worse before they got better. That was a hard conversation."

Governance of the not-for-profit ThedaCare stipulated that four trustees were
family physicians, four were specialists and eight members were chosen from
outside industries. It was from those eight industry leaders – all of whom had
led or participated in operational excellence transformations – that Dr. Toussaint received his necessary support.

"They said the reason your results are poor is that you're actually trying to do
something. If your results weren't poor, we would probably tell you that you're
not doing it right," Dr. Toussaint said.

The four family physicians on the board were somewhat positive about lean
because there had been early, successful continuous improvement projects in
two clinics. The specialists were a different matter. They had seen no benefits
from lean; they saw the bad results as a warning sign and were willing to agree
that Dr. Toussaint was maybe "wrecking the place."

From that meeting, Dr. Toussaint realized that specialists were deeply unhappy
and suspicious of lean. And it was not just the specialists. For three years,
continuous improvement projects had focused only on the needs of patient-
customers. But in a healthcare system, there are other customers, such as specialists and nurses who were on the front line of care every day. Dr. Toussaint
saw that they also needed a full measure of his attention.

Dr. Toussaint believed, up until that point, that the defection of the eight
orthopedic surgeons was an isolated case. Suddenly, it was clear that he could
have even more disastrous resignations on his hands.

"As leaders, we are often insulated from the truth," Dr. Toussaint said. "Ulti-
mately, we all learned that an important part of courage is self-reflection. We
need to reflect on our actions and impact as individuals, as a team, and we

need system feedback to understand how our ideas are actually affecting others on the wider scale. This requires that we wipe away the hopeful feelings we have and see what actually is."

As a result of that meeting, Dr. Toussaint became even more committed to surveys, open-ended employee meetings, and going to gemba. Going to gemba, he said, is the most important kind of self-reflection a leader can do. If one truly listens, and asks questions of the front-line employees, the truth cannot help but be revealed.

In Dr. Toussaint's experience, a front-line nurse is almost always willing to tell a CEO exactly what she or he thinks about the ways things are being run. To stay and really listen is a degree of courage all its own.

Of course, this does not mean that we change policies or switch courses with every bit of feedback. True courage is often best illustrated by a leader's willingness to remain true to his or her principles, beyond what the most recent polls or surveys say.

Politicians are handed a massive dose of system reflection with every campaign. And in the run up to the general election of 1864, Abraham Lincoln struggled mightily with his principles and his popularity.

After signing the executive order titled the Emancipation Proclamation on January 1, 1863, the debate surrounding the on-going Civil War had shifted dramatically. What had been a war to remake a Union shattered by Confederate guns at Fort Sumter had slowly become a war about slavery. As brothers and cousins faced each other on bloody battlefields, families lost a generation of men, and riots broke out surrounding anti-draft demonstrations, people asked why they fought. And many were reluctant or opposed to dying for people of a different skin color, no matter how sorely they had been abused.

In Lincoln's own party, Republicans were split between those who supported the war effort and those who thought Lincoln should have freed all slaves, immediately. The Democrats were divided between the radical Copperheads, who wanted an immediate cessation of fighting even if it split the country in two, and the War Democrats who supported a war for the sake of the Union, but not necessarily for an end to slavery.

In the summer of 1864, the Democrats appeared to find a man to rally behind in the person of Gen. George B. McClellan. Fired by Lincoln for inaction during the terrible battles of 1862, McClellan was courted to become the Presidential challenger by powerful Democrats in New York. At an enormous rally in Times Square that was lit by fireworks and serenaded by cannons, speakers denounced Lincoln for "perverting" the Union cause into an abolitionist fight.

Lincoln's troubles intensified in August when he approved Horace Greeley's request to publish the president's open letter that "conceded that peace was impossible unless the Rebels agreed to free the slaves and remake the Union."[81]

This was not a sudden shift, of course. The historian Richard Carwardine described it best: "Over sixteen months, by increments, Lincoln had moved. From firmly repudiating emancipation as a weapon of war, he had moved to declare the advancing Union forces the liberators of millions in bondage. From tolerating the return of fugitive slaves to Rebel masters, he had moved to invite freed men to take up arms against those who had shackled them. From defining the war's purpose as the reestablishment of a Union committed to no more than a gradual melting away of the peculiar institution, he had moved to champion a nation energized by the prospect of slavery's imminent and permanent removal."[82]

The Lincoln letter published by Greeley still took many by surprise. Democrats called it proof that Lincoln had hijacked the war effort "in the interest of the black race."[83] Writing in a Green Bay, Wisconsin, newspaper, Editor Charles Robinson said that Lincoln's letter "takes us War Democrats clear off our feet." Alerted by Wisconsin Governor Alexander Randall to the Green Bay editorial – and the very real possibility of losing the huge voting block

81. Michael Beschloss, *Presidential Courage: Brave Leaders and How They Changed America 1789-1989* (Simon & Schuster, 2008) 115
82. Richard Carwardine, *Lincoln: A Life of Purpose and Power* (Alfred A. Knopf, 2006) 220
83. Beschloss, *Presidential Courage.* 116

of so-called War Democrats – Lincoln began writing a letter in response to Robinson's editorial.

This was in the heat of the final days of August. Lincoln was staying in a cottage at the Soldiers' Home in Washington, D.C., while his wife and sons were away on vacation. In a draft of that letter to the Wisconsin editor, Lincoln appeared to hedge his bets, to attempt to appease Democrats by saying that his position was not necessarily full emancipation or nothing. "If Jefferson Davis wishes to know what I would do if he were to offer peace and re-union, saying nothing about slavery, let him try me," Lincoln wrote.[84] It was a delicate, not-entirely-honest dance of words.

The tension between the two poles – staying true to principles versus responding to the needs and beliefs, even the prejudices, of the people we lead – can drive a leader to greatness or ruin. Again, it is principles versus popularity. John Toussaint faced this while standing up to his peers regarding medical errors, and then in front of his Board of Trustees with his terrible survey results, asking to continue the lean journey. Should a leader stick to his guns, even as others turn against him or her and it is not clear who is right? When is compromise the better course?

In the midst of a full internal debate, Lincoln turned to his friend Frederick Douglass, described the predicament and showed him a draft of the Robinson letter. Douglass denounced the letter, calling it a "complete surrender of your anti-slavery policy." The letter was not sent. Lincoln, it seemed, chose to stay with his anti-slavery principles and invited Gov. Randall to visit his cottage at the Soldiers' Home.

Lincoln reminded Randall that the Emancipation Proclamation had allowed some 200,000 freed slaves to join the Union Army and that, without those brave men, the Northern army would not be faring nearly as well. If Lincoln tried to placate the South by returning those free men to the former masters, Lincoln said, he would be "damned in time and eternity."[85]

---

84. ibid
85. ibid

Courageous

For a time, it seemed as though his principles would cost Lincoln dearly. Holding court at his summer cottage in those weeks, Lincoln was visited by one depressive political operative after another. The heat and the steady stream of bad news were obviously wearying the president. One visitor urged him to get some rest, to "play hermit for a fortnight."

"Ah, two or three weeks would do me no good. I cannot fly from my thoughts," Lincoln replied.[86]

Leonard Swett, an old friend who had engineered Lincoln's 1860 Presidential nomination, told Lincoln that, under current conditions, he could not hope to carry even three states. And then, Lincoln's luck turned.

On August 29th, at the Democratic Convention in Chicago, the radical Copperhead wing of the party successfully pushed a platform demanding an immediate end to Lincoln's war "experiment." The South, they said, did not even need to re-enter the Union. It was, in effect, an unconditional surrender. Gen. McClellan, the presidential nominee who had run on the promise that peace was contingent on restoration of the Union, declared that he could not endorse his own party's platform.

Then on September 1, Gen. William T. Sherman's army marched into Atlanta and lit up the city. Sherman cabled Lincoln a single line: "So Atlanta is ours, and fairly won."

Two weeks later, Gen. Philip Sheridan wiped the Rebel Jubal Early's troops out of the Shenandoah. Two months later, Lincoln won re-election, was assured of winning the war, and began putting his political weight behind passage of the 13th Amendment to the Constitution, outlawing slavery throughout the nation.

Had he lost the courage of his convictions, Lincoln would have appeared just as disjointed as the Democratic Party and its leader. It is almost impossible to calculate what all of us would have lost as a result.

---

86. Beschloss, *Presidential Courage.* 119

Every leader seeking transformational change will likely be tempted to back-slide to a more popular position at one point or another along the journey. But a courageous leader does not think about personal consequences. He thinks about what might happen to his organization if she fails to make change.

Here we arrive at another one of those tension points, this one between the leader who courageously sticks to her guns and one who is indomitably stubborn. I suspect that most of us have danced back and forth across this line as we have tried to convince an organization that a new direction is needed. Sometimes, a good bit of pushing and pulling is required.

For myself, I am sure that I crossed that line more than once for what I believed was a worthy cause: bringing lean improvements to the people. Leaders who have not yet begun a lean transformation should probably be warned about this phenomenon. Seeing and being part of a lean transformation can have a profound effect on a person. Some of us become a bit fanatical.

In the years after Medtronic began humming along as a lean operation – still making big leaps in quality improvements and resources savings, but more stable and sure – I started itching to introduce these ideas to others. Around Jacksonville, I saw a lot of businesses struggling. Worthy non-profit organizations were going under as money dried up in the years after 9/11. Our schools were not doing well. Knowing that I would retire in Jacksonville, I started thinking about my responsibility to give back to this community.

I started in my own metaphoric backyard. As a member of the Board of Directors for the First Coast Manufacturing Association, I had a little bit of a bully pulpit for my ideas. At least, I thought I did. The association was always looking for ways to deliver value to its member organizations and I knew the perfect project: a consortium of companies that would help one another learn lean thinking and apply it in their businesses. Eventually, the consortium would reach beyond the manufacturing world to include charities, schools and local governments – any organization that needed to cut waste and improve performance. I was on fire with this idea, absolutely certain that the other board members would rally around. I gave an impassioned presentation on the idea to my fellow board members.

There was silence. I waited. Then someone cleared his throat and moved on to the next order of business.

I was stunned and a little bit sheepish. But over the next week or so, in reflecting on the idea, I became convinced all over again that this was the right thing to do. It was not for me; it was for Jacksonville. So the next month, I gave the lean consortium pitch all over again. This time, I earned a few smiles from other board members. Some people shook their heads or looked away. But that was OK. Next month, I vowed, they would listen.

Over time, one board member here or there would ask me after the meeting to describe this *lean thinking* I was always on about. Lad Daniels, president of the association, encouraged me to keep bringing it up. Months went by and I kept giving my pitch. After a full year of this, month in and month out, one board member finally said, "Jerry, if we do this, will you shut up about it?"

"Sure," I said. By this time, I had the full attention of Chipper Hall, president and owner of Rex Packaging Inc., who became an early advocate. We arranged a series of business breakfasts that were meant to be awareness raising and found that many members knew continuous improvement on an ad hoc basis, but not as a system-wide initiative, so that is where I focused attention.

Still looking for a more inclusive and cohesive program, I kept talking up the idea of a Jacksonville Consortium to anyone who would listen. Invited to give my presentation to a forum of local businesses that were hearing an official from the National Football League talk about the Super Bowl that year, I prepared for a big audience and walked into a room that contained nothing but a mop. A few people did trickle in, however, and one of those people, Bruce Ferguson, helped the Consortium get its first real break in the form of funding from the state Department of Labor's WorkSource program.

With $375,000 in seed money, we began to organize with the help of David

Chao who ran the Vancouver Consortium and in mid-2003, we launched the FCMA Jacksonville Lean Consortium. That first year, 16 companies joined. The second year, another 16 were added. After the setbacks of the Great Recession, the Consortium has been holding steady at 42-48 member organizations, each of them striving to help others and to become more lean.

The Consortium was there when Sheriff John Rutherford was looking for a way to cut waste – and eliminate siphoning of public funds – in his administration in order to put more resources into crime fighting. New Heights of Northeast Florida (formerly United Cerebral Palsy of Northeast Florida) joined us when it was looking to expand its mission of service in tight financial times. Consortium members were there for my dentist, Dr. Sami Bahri, as he was there for others, as they tried to translate lean principles in an unfamiliar environment. And when Safariland – a major manufacturer of law enforcement security products – needed to increase its production of bulletproof vests, Consortium members were there to help. Using lean principles, teams at Safariland were able to nearly double the output of the bulletproof vest line.

Once a month, we do gemba walks in one of the member companies. Members who master a skill or concept turn around and offer training to others. Our Consortium staff is small – just 2.5 full-time employees – but it is working. And the idea seems to be growing; two consortiums have begun in Texas and another one in Chicago.

As director emeritus of the Jacksonville Consortium, I have stepped back my involvement some, but am still hoping to get lean into the schools, to help cut administrative waste and bring some new training ideas into the mix. Lean's focus on the scientific method, on visual management and organization would be an invaluable addition to higher-level curriculums, where students could learn to work on teams and engage in creative problem solving. Even younger students could benefit from lean. But so far, that has been a tough nut to crack. People still like to tell me that it is a crazy idea and just will not work.

Lean leaders need to be prepared to hear that sort of thing. It seems as though there are always naysayers hanging around at the starting line of a lean initia-

Courageous

tive. Some people want lean to fail because they are afraid of change. Others worry that lean will grab up whatever scarce resources are available, leaving less for them and their concerns. What they do not know is that lean, done right and led intelligently, frees up more resources for all. That is just one of the reasons why strong leadership is so vital to a lean transformation: keeping the naysayers from taking over the conversation.

In the usually rocky beginning of a lean conversion, a good leader will not just be courageous; he or she will look for and cultivate the courage in others. None of us operate in isolation, after all, and the strength of a leader should be judged by the strength of strength of the organization.

Five Questions on Courageous Leadership

1. Describe a situation in your professional or personal life in which you exhibited a substantial amount of courage?
2. What are some of the factors that discourage you and others in your organization from being courageous?
3. How do you encourage your direct reports and others to be courageous when necessary?
4. Name a personal role model for courageous behavior and describe how that person is courageous, and how he or she influences your actions.
5. Do you consciously decide to be courageous and, if so, what are the mental steps you take in deciding to employ courageous behavior?

WHAT'S NEXT?

Practice being the leader you want to be. Accept failures and learn from them. Analyze new situations and identify the results you seek. Practice more.

Management guru Ken Blanchard once stated, "Knowledge without application doesn't mean squat." As a basketball player, I found that the only way I became a better rebounder was to work very hard at practicing the skills that I was taught by my coaches. I work the same way to this day as I try to hone my leadership skills. It takes personal commitment, knowledge, a great deal of discipline, many hours of practice and hard work to excel at leadership.

As in sports, it is very important to have the assistance of a coach to help you with areas where you need improvement and provide reinforcement for those things that you are doing well. It is also essential to have the trust and support of members on your team. Mutual accountability and peer pressure are critical ingredients in helping you stay the course through challenging times and continue on the path to achieving your objectives.

There is no single formula or recipe to follow. Early in my lean journey, I looked for a prescription that would make me an effective lean leader. I learned through hard experience that it does work that way. A lean leadership pill would be really cool if it worked, but in reality there are no shortcuts. There is practice, more practice, and learning from experience.

Malcolm Gladwell, in his book *Outliers*,[87] described the critical impact of practice in a chapter titled "The 10,000-Hour Rule." Gladwell wrote, "The idea

---

87. Malcolm Gladwell, *Outliers: The Story of Success* (Little, Brown and Company, 2008)

that excellence at performing a complex task requires a critical minimum level of practice surfaces again and again in studies of expertise. In fact, researchers have settled on what they believe is the magic number for true expertise: Ten thousand hours."

Gladwell detailed the practice habits of highly successful individuals from a wide range of fields, such as Bill Gates of Microsoft Corp. and the musicians who formed The Beatles, in successfully testing the point of ten thousand hours of practice. In reflecting on my own experience transitioning from traditional leadership to the significantly different behaviors of a lean leader, I have to say that the 10,000-Hour Rule appears to be on the mark. To become a lean leader is to learn by doing. Some of the most profound learning comes through failures. Developing expertise in lean leadership takes dedication and years of hard work.

It also takes character. As I described earlier in this book, I have discovered that good lean leaders have specific character traits in common. I identified 10 of those traits, demonstrated here with the stories of Abraham Lincoln and highly successful CEOs. It certainly is not the simple formulae that I originally sought. But I know for certain that these characteristics can all be learned through repetition. The average person may not ever be able to execute a good jump shot or play the violin, but through desire and effort, one can be respectful, honest, persistent, courageous and every other characteristic. I hope that these illustrations will help leaders define their goals, and to picture the behaviors they seek to create in order to practice becoming that leader.

There are also practical applications I can recommend. I learned a long time ago that lean leaders should never provide prepackaged answers. We must help others discover the answers through supplying good questions, and perhaps by sharing stories and experiences that may help stimulate ideas. So, it might be helpful if I shared a practice that I followed with my teams over many years.

When I came across very special books that contained information I thought could help us to enhance our lean leadership capabilities, we followed a standard process. During monthly staff meetings, we set aside 30 minutes to cover one chapter of a leadership book we were all reading. Two team members would present the key points of the chapter and, when appropriate, would describe how some points applied to themselves and the team. We encouraged everyone to interject creativity and humor into presentations to make learning fun. This approach was very effective in adopting concepts from books such as *The 7 Habits of Highly Effective People, The Eighth Habit, Emotional Intelligence, Good to Great* and *Lincoln on Leadership.* Often we spent the entire year sharing, learning and applying the key points from a single book. In terms of the *7 Habits,* we worked on sharpening the saw every year. After studying the Socratic method, we introduced that kind of questioning into our presentations, as well.

Over the years, I discovered that changing behaviors was really hard for me and for others in the organization – even if we knew exactly how we wanted to change. We tried to deliver many different types of training sessions, utilizing various methodologies and coaching programs with limited success. Our success rate with 360-degree evaluations and other leadership performance reviews was low. An individual might change a little, but those changes were rarely sustained. Finally, however, we did find a leadership performance review that proved to be robust and sustainable.

We called the process Red Card/Green Card. A value stream manager, for example, would distribute a red and green index card to each of her or his direct reports. On the red index card, the subordinate listed two specific ways that the value stream manager was failing to meet expectations. On the green card, the subordinate listed two good behaviors. The team members did not put their names on either card, which were then reviewed by the leader's boss and a representative from Human Resources. The two most common behavioral themes were selected from the red and green cards.

Then, the value stream leader would meet with his or her boss to review the results and prepare an A3. The A3 focused on counter measures to the red-card traits in order to create an improvement plan. We also looked at green-card traits, of course, and talked about how to increase the frequency of those behaviors. That A3 would then hang in the leader's area where he and his direct reports would review it monthly for progress.

After 90 days, the process would be repeated with new red and green index cards. Whether or not the same good and bad traits were repeated, a new A3 plan would be prepared. This was an on-going lean leadership development journey; it did not end.

A more individual approach I used to reinforce mutual accountability consisted of Saturday morning sessions with my brother, Paul, at Starbucks. Paul is the CEO of New Heights, a non-profit in Jacksonville, and he has spent most of his career in the non-profit sector. After moving to Jacksonville, Paul and his organization joined the Jacksonville Lean Consortium as New Heights was always looking for better ways to benefit clients with disabilities. For three years, we met for coffee almost every Saturday morning.

What began as a social event became an opportunity for professional growth as I found how beneficial it is to spend time on a regular basis with a fellow lean leader discussing our approaches, challenges, lessons learned, failures and successes. Mutual trust is a key ingredient, of course, and it may take some networking to find a respected equal. Taking the time to find such a leadership partner is, however, time well spent. Never underestimate the power of peer pressure. Of course, we do not spend all of or our time at Starbucks talking about leadership. We give plenty of airtime to sports and trying to solve the problems of the world each week. But we have also made it a point to carve out sufficient time to discuss lean leadership, asking questions of one another and listening carefully.

Certainly I have a unique situation my brother. We have great relationship, live in the same town and share a passion for lean thinking and leadership. Still, I would urge every lean leader to seek a friend in the same position for feedback on a regular basis. Paul has been a huge help to me as I seek to state and stay the course, achieving our objectives.

One final approach I want to discuss is leadership standard work. Companies that are serious about the lean journey have begun adopting standard work for leaders, all the way up the chain to presidents and directors. In most cases, standard work has focused on scheduling. At Medtronic, my standard work sheet spanned a month and included a set number of gemba walks, coaching sessions, the use of Socratic questions, etc. One of my direct reports would be responsible for reviewing my standard work sheets and making sure I met all my goals. At other companies, standard work has been used to ensure that leaders are available to their subordinates at reliable times to assist people and processes. When done well, standard work includes set-aside time for coaching and specific mentoring goals.

Keeping leaders to standard work is not easy. Everyone claims that they need a large amount of scheduling flexibility in order to firefight. Just like the physical processes of a shop floor, however, leadership work can be simpler and involve fewer fires once there is more predictability in the work content. Using a process like Red Card/Green Card along with standard work, I believe, is useful in promoting accountability and transparency, and promoting steady improvement, in leadership work.

Above all these great ideas, however, there is the one that began this book and to which we must return: purpose. If there is one thing that a reader takes away from this book, I hope it is that purpose – the single compelling vision of what the organization is trying to achieve – is the key. Every other character trait is in support of the unifying sense of being purposeful.

Purpose is about reaching for something larger than us, and then sharing that vision with others. It is a great gift to imbue others with larger goals and grander themes. Lean thinking offers everyone in an organization the opportunity to be involved in transformation – in significant, lasting change. It is a rare opportunity in a world where too many people feel undervalued and overlooked.

As a leader, mentoring people to do more than they thought possible has been one of my greatest satisfactions. Helping people step out of comfort zones, helping them to see failure as a first step toward learning, and to see their efforts as contributing to something larger, has given me greater purpose, as well. This never would have been possible in a command-and-control environment. And knowing that I've made a difference in people's lives has made all the difference.

ACKNOWLEDGMENTS

During my business career I have been very fortunate because of all the op-portunities I received to constantly learn from so many people. There have been literally thousands of people I have either learned from or collaborated with in solving problems and engaging in continuous improvement. It is obvi-ously impossible for me to acknowledge everyone on an individual basis. There is a large group of people who I feel compelled to mention by name. For those not mentioned who have been very helpful to me, please accept my sincere thanks and gratitude.

First of all I want to thank UL for agreeing to provide the financial support and resources that enabled this book to be written, published, promoted and distributed. Special thanks to Juan Amador at UL for believing in the impor-tance of producing this book and for gaining approval from the decision mak-ers there. I would also like to express my gratitude to Keith Williams, CEO of UL, Patrick Boyle, president of UL's Knowledge Services business, and Scot Webster, senior vice president of Global Operations, for their encouragement, support and friendship.

At UL, the point person in providing support to me on this project was Val Liberman. Val was able to ensure everything required from UL was completed in an effective and very timely fashion. It was a real pleasure working with Val because anything I gave to him was taken care of properly and there was no need for follow up. Val, thanks so much for everything you did to make sure we met all our objectives. I also want to thank Natasha LaBruce, Megan Madrid and Lisa Stern at UL for all their help and the time they dedicated to this project.

Acknowledgments

I was very fortunate to be able to convince Emily Adams, an incredibly gifted writer to collaborate with me in producing this book. Emily has previously been involved with other authors in writing books around lean thinking. The depth of her experience made this project flow very smoothly. Emily provided one-stop shopping, from helping me to outline the book through getting the book produced on schedule. Emily, thanks for making this whole process a very enjoyable learning and communications journey. We received tremendous assistance around researching Lincoln stories and topics from Psyche Pascual, who was diligent and resourceful in repeatedly finding just the right information. Thanks to Laurie Anderson for her keen editing eye; she consistently made us better on the page. We also found exactly the right creative person in Tom Adams to design the book jacket. His ability to take concepts and turn them into exceptional images is amazing. Thanks, Tom, for doing a wonderful job on the book jacket.

My friend Jim Womack graciously agreed to do the editing for this book. He provided us with numerous insightful comments and questions. In the spirit of continuous improvement we were able to take his comments and make very positive changes to improve the book. I also want to express my gratitude to you, Jim, for all I have learned from you through your books, epistles, materials, sessions produced by the Lean Enterprise Institute and through direct personal interactions with you. I look forward to continuing to learn from you.

To the 10 current or former CEOs who were interviewed for the book and shared their experiences, I want to express my gratitude. They all were very accommodating and willing to openly express their insights, stories and lessons. It was pretty remarkable how they all fit us into to their busy schedules and provided quick feedback on written material. Gentlemen, thanks so much for your special contributions to this book.

There are quite a few highly respected people who I asked to read the draft of this book and to provide their reactions and feedback. Thank you to the following individuals who generously agreed to help: Jeff Liker, John Shook, Dave Hogg, Mark Graban, Mike Hoseus, Ross Robson, Bruce Hamilton, Jim Huntzinger, Cliff Ransom, Bob Wood, Helen Zak, Peter Ward, Doug Carlberg, Dave McKinley, Frank Williams, Mark Siwik, Doc Hall, Craig Long and Dr. Sami Bahri.

I want to extend a very special thank you to my good friend Ross Robson, the former executive director of the Shingo organization. Ross introduced the Shingo model to me at a training session during a Shingo Conference in Columbus, Ohio. He whet my appetite for gaining an understanding of lean thinking and introduced me to many helpful people during the early years of my lean journey. I will always also be very grateful to you, Ross, for asking me to join the Shingo Board of Governors. It continues to be a great learning experience and way to help others succeed on their lean journeys.

In forming the Jacksonville Lean Consortium I was able to partner with Lad Daniels, former president of the First Coast Manufacturers Association, who is one of the finest civic leaders in the Jacksonville community. Over the years Lad opened many important doors. Thanks, Lad, for your example, mentorship, support and friendship.

I also want to recognize the excellent leaders who helped to build, grow and sustain the Jacksonville Lean Consortium. Thank you for all of your efforts, Amy Erickson, David Chao, Joe Rizzo, Bob Golitz and our great friend the late Mike Houle. Special thanks also to a very active Board of Directors.

In terms of lean leadership, I have learned more from John Shook than any individual in the lean community. In conversation, formal presentation, and the books *Learning to See* and *Managing to Learn*, you have been incredibly helpful to my journey. John: Thanks for your support and friendship.

I have learned a great deal from Mike Hoseus, Toyota veteran and author of *The Toyota Culture*. Mike's workshops covering Toyota's philosophy, business practices, leadership and the eight-step problem solving methodology were all very valuable learning sessions. Thanks Mike for sharing generously and for your friendship.

Also I want to acknowledge David Chao, the President of Lean Sensei Inter-

Acknowledgments

national, for all I learned from him during the early years of my lean journey and for a great learning experience together in Japan. Thank you David.

There are so many people who I had the pleasure to work with during our lean journey at Medtronic. Emmanuel Dujarric was the key champion during our initial lean efforts in France and has become an exceptional lean leader. Jon Swanson played a major role in helping us get lean up off the ground in Jacksonville and made notable contributes at different stages of our lean journey. The following individuals stayed the course and were the truly committed to contributing in different ways to enable lean to be successful at our various facilities. Thank You Debra Rosamilia, Scott Quaratella, Curt Nunier, Chuck Carlton, Nicolas Deflandre, Barney Carter, Marie Garnes, and Ben Rubin. Mike Nicoletta, Rick Kundert, Mark Himes, Don Healy, Ken Wise, Jeff Pfeiffer, Doug Francis, Darron Barnwell, Rose Madrid, Manny Patel, Tim Romecki, Chad Tremaroli, Gary Steen, Corrine Dujarric, Darron Barnwell, Rose Madrid, David Frank, Rick Brandl, Wolfgang Krull, Inez Anderson and Judith Fisher. Also thanks to the following individuals who I worked with to help promote the Shingo model and conduct assessments across Medtronic operations: Greg Johnson, Andy Kinser, Martin Conroy, Jeff Hans, Dave Cano and Mike Larsen.

Special thanks to Margaret Kennedy at Medtronic who inspired me regularly through her caring attitude, exceptional customer service and ability to demonstrate genuine respect for people.

Dr. Sami Bahri, thanks for being a great role model for lean leadership, continuous learning and persistence. I am very grateful for the regular opportunities to have very meaningful conversations with you and for our special friendship.

Over the years there have many good friends who have listened to and endured my stories about lean thinking, Lincoln and the book project. Thanks for your patience and understanding: Wally and Sue Wisniewski, Jimmy and Fern Alexanderson, Tom and Pam Schneider, Randy and Janice Bennett, Fred Pruitt, Dr. B.J. Barakat, Dr. Gary Snyder, Hayward Riiser, Steve Gilbert, Rich Karn, Paul Rochester, Mike Sims, Alan Verlander, Greg Strong, Murat Tiryakioglu, John Osgathorpe, the staff at my local Starbucks and the one and only Thomas Worthington III.

I want to thank my mother and father Marie and Gerry Bussell for their love and being supportive throughout their lives. I am very grateful for the important lessons learned and the help I received from my sister Barbara and my brother Brian during their lives. I feel very fortunate that my brother Paul and I are able to maintain a very close relationship and continue to look out for one another. It is great to add lean to the long list of things we both enjoy doing.

I also want to acknowledge my mother-in-law Helen Fortune who celebrated her 90th birthday earlier this year and my father-in-law the late Hank Fortune. They both have always made me feel that they were very proud of the work I was doing as a leader and recognized my career successes in special ways.

I want to thank my daughter Brianne for her patience with me throughout the zealous years of my lean journey. When Brianne was 16 years old she stated, "If Daddy says the word *lean* one more time I am going to scream." Today she shares with me how different processes she observes could be improved dramatically through the application of lean. I am so proud of what she is doing in her personal life, with her marriage this year to Rick Cartlidge, and her success in her professional career. My son James is a really good person and I am very proud of him as he begins his career in law; we also are currently having some fun working together on a very challenging lean project.

Finally and most importantly, I want to express my love and thanks to my wife Mary. She has been my mentor and sensei. Mary has helped me in so many ways to become a better person and a much better leader. Thanks Mary, for your love and for who you are.

Bibliography

David Acord, *What Would Lincoln Do? Lincoln's Most Inspired Solutions to Challenging Problems and Difficult Situations* (Sourcebooks, 2009)

Dr. Sami Bahri, *Follow the Learner: The Role of a Leader in Creating a Lean Culture* (Lean Enterprise Institute, 2009)

Warren Bennis, *On Becoming a Leader* (Basic Books, Addison-Wesley, 1989)

Michael Beschloss, *Presidential Courage: Brave Leaders and How They Changed America 1789-1989* (Simon & Schuster, 2007)

Marcus Buckingham and Curt Coffman, *First Break All the Rules: What the World's Greatest Managers Do Differently* (Simon & Schuster, 1999)

Nick Bunker, "The Top 10 Middle-Class Acts of Congress: Laws That Helped Our Country Prosper," The Center For American Progress, accessed July 2, 2012, http://www.americanprogress.org/issues/2012/01/middle_class_acts.html

Michael Burlingame, *Lincoln and the Civil War* (Southern Illinois University Press, 2011)

Art Byrne, *The Lean Turnaround: How Business Leaders Use Lean Principles to Create Value and Transform Their Company* (McGraw-Hill, 2012)

Richard Carwardine, *Lincoln: A Life of Purpose and Power* (Alfred Knopf, 2006)

Jim Collins, and Morten T. Hansen, *Good to Great: Why Some Companies Make the Leap...and Others Don't* (HarperCollins, 2001)

Bibliography

Jim Collins, Morten T. Hansen, *Great by Choice: Uncertainty, Chaos, and Luck – Why Some Thrive Despite Them All* (HarperCollins, 2011)

Stephen Covey, *The 7 Habits of Highly Effective People* (Free Press, 1989)

Stephen Covey, *The 8th Habit: From Effectiveness to Greatness* (Free Press, 2004)

Max De Pree, *Leadership is an Art* (Dell Publishing, 1989)

Charles Duhigg, *The Power of Habit: Why We Do What We Do in Life and Business* (Random House, 2012)

Eric Foner, *Our Lincoln: New Perspectives on Lincoln and His World* (W.W. Norton & Co., 2008)

Bill George, *Authentic Leadership: Rediscovering the Secrets to Creating Lasting Value* (Jossey-Bass, 2003)

Gary Giroux and Sharon Johns, "Financing The Civil War: The Office of Internal Revenue and Use of Revenue Stamps." Paper, Texas A&M University Department of Accounting, April 2000, accessed May 16, 2012. http://web.acct.tamu.edu/giroux/financingcivtl.htm

Doris Kearns Goodwin, *Team of Rivals: The Political Genius of Abraham Lincoln* (Simon & Schuster, 2005)

Daniel Goleman, *Emotional Intelligence* (Bantam Books, 1995)

Robert K. Greenleaf, *Servant Leadership: A Journey into the Nature of Legitimate Power and Greatness* (Paulist Press, 1977)

David Hirsch and Dan Van Haften, *Abraham Lincoln and the Structure of Reason* (Savas Beatie, 2010)

Richard Hofstader, *Great Issues in American History, Vol. II: From the Revolution to the Civil War, 1765-1865* (Vintage Books, 1958)

Joseph Jaworski and Peter M. Senge, *Synchronicity: The Inner Path of Leadership* (Berrett-Koehler, 1996)

Robert J. Johnson, *Trial by Fire: Abraham Lincoln and the Law* (ProQuest, 2007)

Daniel T. Jones and James P. Womack, *Seeing the Whole: Mapping the Extended Value Stream* (Lean Enterprise Institute, 2002)

Wilmer L. Jones, *Generals in Blue and Gray: Vol. 1 Lincoln's Generals* (Greenwood, 2004)

William K. Klingaman, *Abraham Lincoln and the Road to Emancipation 1861-1865* (Viking Penguin, 2001)

George Koenigsaecker, *Leading the Lean Enterprise Transformation,* (Productivity Press, 2009)

John P. Kotter and Dan S. Cohen, *The Heart of Change: Real-Life Stories of How People Change Their Organizations* (Harvard Business Review Press, 2002)

James M. Kouzes and Barry Z. Posner, *The Leadership Challenge* (Jossey-Bass, 2002)

Abraham Lincoln, edited by H. Jack Lang, *The Original Wit & Wisdom of Abraham Lincoln: As Reflected in His Letters and Speeches* (Stackpole Books, 2006)

Abraham Lincoln, Henry Jarvis Raymond and Francis Bicknell, *Lincoln, His Life And Times V1: Being The Life And Public Services Of Abraham Lincoln, Sixteenth President Of The United States* (1891) (Nabu Press, 2011)

Bibliography

Abraham Lincoln, "Full Text Abraham Lincoln Cooper Union Address" *The New York Times*, 2004. Available at: http://www.nytimes.com/2004/05/02/nyregion/03lincoln-text.html

William Marvel, *Lincoln's Darkest Year: The War In 1862* (Houghton Mifflin Harcourt, 2008)

George S. McGovern, *Abraham Lincoln, The American Presidents Series: The 16th President 1861-1865* (Times Books, 2008)

Ralph Y. McGinnis and Calvin N. Smith, *Abraham Lincoln and the Western Territories* (Rowman & Littlefield, 1994)

James M. McPherson, *Tried By War: Abraham Lincoln As Commander in Chief* (Penguin Press, 2008)

James M. McPherson, *Abraham Lincoln* (Oxford University Press, 2009)

Richard Lawrence Miller, *Lincoln and His World: Volume 4, The Path to the Presidency 1854-1860* (McFarland & Co., 2012)

Michael Perman and Amy Murrell Taylor, *Major Problems in the Civil War and Reconstruction: Documents and Essays* (Wadsworth Publishing, 2011)

Donald T. Phillips II, *Lincoln on Leadership: Executive Strategies for Tough Times* (Warner Books, 1992)

Lance H. K. Secretan, *Inspire! What Great Leaders Do* (John Wiley & Sons, 2004)

Shigeo Shingo, *Kaizen and the Art of Creative Thinking – The Scientific Thinking Mechanism* (Enna Products Corporation, 2007)

John Toussaint, MD, *Potent Medicine: The Collaborative Cure for Healthcare* (ThedaCare Center for Healthcare Value, 2012)

John Toussaint, MD and Roger A. Gerard, Ph.D., *On the Mend: Revolutionizing Healthcare to Save Lives and Transform The Industry* (Lean Enterprise Institute, 2010)

James P. Womack and Daniel T. Jones, *Lean Thinking: Banish Waste and Create Wealth in Your Corporation* (Simon & Schuster, 1996)

Steven E. Woodworth, Kenneth J. Winkle and James McPherson, *Oxford Atlas of the Civil War* (Oxford University Press, 2004)

Index

Index